Once, feeling sorry for an emerging b
remaining tendons. The wing muscles remained undeveloped
and the butterfly never flew. This superb book gives you the
right formula to empower your kids from the start and raise
them up to be bright, resourceful, happy adults and truly let
them fly.

—Dr. Stephen R. Covey, author
The 7 Habits of Highly Effective People

Excellent book! Want to raise kids who grow up happy, successful, and confident? The essential ingredient, often over-
looked by parents who are busy trying to accomplish so much
for their children, is found in this book. In no time at all your
kids will go from "I can't" to "I can!"

—Dr. Paul Coleman, author
*How to Say It to Your Kids! The Right Words to
Solve Problems, Soothe Feelings, and Teach Values*

Smart Parenting is a truly excellent book. The authors have
nailed the problem: kids are NOT born self-reliant. Parents and
teachers will love the fun activities that teach children self-
reliance. I endorse this book wholeheartedly because it fits perfectly with our philosophy—advocating respectful ways to
teach children valuable life skills.

—Dr. Jane Nelsen, author
*Positive Discipline, Raising Self-Reliant Children
in a Self-Indulgent World,* and *From Here to Serenity*

Smart Parenting is a "smart" parenting book. The authors provide you with a terrific set of tools for connecting and communicating with your children. *Smart Parenting* is just the right
blend of advice and tactics for building self-esteem in your kids
and feeling great about being a "smart" parent. Read it, apply
it, and you just may help your children grow into confident people who navigate well through the maze of life.

—Steve Bennett, co-author
365 TV-Free Activities You Can Do With Your Child

At any age, children are as old as they've ever been. If they don't feel capable—able to decide things, fix things and find energy and curiosity from within—how can they grow with the enthusiasm and confidence that every parent hopes for? Brad and Kate's inspiring book focuses on the source of true happiness: encouraging children to develop the skills and attitudes that enable them to make things happen and really live their lives rather than be a passive and disengaged spectator. *Smart Parenting* is fun to read, full of practical games that show parents what to do and should be read widely.

—Elizabeth Hartley-Brewer, author
Raising a Self-starter, Raising Confident Boys
and *Raising Confident Girls*

SMART PARENTING

How to Raise Happy, Can-Do Kids

DR. BRAD SMART and
DR. KATE SMART MURSAU

CDK Press
Wadsworth, Illinois

9 8 7 6 5 4 3 2 1   10 09 08 07 06

ISBN 0-9777044-0-8

Production and editorial services provided by CWL Publishing Enterprises, Inc., Madison, Wisconsin, www.cwlpub.com.

Cover design by Greg Paus.

CDK Press
37202 North Black Velvet Lane
Wadsworth, IL 60083

For answers to questions, sharing Smart Parenting experiences, downloading (free) the SMART Decision Pad, or ordering multiple copies of *Smart Parenting* at a discount, go to **www.AskSmartParenting.com.**

DEDICATION

To the next generation of can-do kids—
Will, Kendall, and Andrew, and more to come!
—Brad

To my husband, Chris, for your unconditional love and support.
—Kate

CONTENTS

Acknowledgments   ix

Foreword   xi

Introduction   xiii

Part One   **Smart Parenting Building Blocks**
                   for Parents   **1**

Chapter 1   Enjoy the Magic of Smart Parenting   3

Chapter 2   Coach Your Child to Become
                   a Great Decision Maker   17

Chapter 3   Listen to Your Child   32

Chapter 4   Have Meals Together   37

Part Two   **Smart Parenting Activities for Kids**   **51**

Chapter 5   Learn Something Together   53

Chapter 6   Imagine It, Plan It, Build It   67

Chapter 7   Fix Something Together   75

Chapter 8   Learn to Discipline Yourself   82

Chapter 9   Enjoy Weekends Away!   96

Chapter 10   Be a Navigator   106

Chapter 11   Understand How Others See You   115

Chapter 12   Introduce Yourself and Start a Conversation   121

CONTENTS

Chapter 13	Learn Active Listening	128
Chapter 14	Find Ways to Make Friends	136
Chapter 15	Learn Public Speaking	142
Chapter 16	Be a Team Player	147
Chapter 17	Be a Leader	154
Chapter 18	Spot a Winner, Spot a Whiner	161
Chapter 19	Look Ahead, Prevent a Problem	167
Chapter 20	Volunteer	173
Chapter 21	Learn to Budget	179
Chapter 22	Invest Early	183
Chapter 23	Stay Calm, Cool, and Collected (No Matter What)	190
Chapter 24	Be Safe	201
Appendix A	Smart Parenting Case Studies	207
Appendix B	Resource Guide and References	215
Index		221

Acknowledgments

SO MANY PEOPLE BELIEVE DEEPLY in this project that to single out a few for our thanks is difficult. Many, many parents tested the activities over the years, and we offer thanks to them and their children for trusting us and offering their valuable insights.

We have been fortunate to have worked with Libby Koponen, whose love of the topic of this book translated into a wonderfully human style, for which the reader can be thankful. Libby came into our families to truly understand the thousand ways parents can show their love by releasing resourcefulness in their children, and her warmth and genuineness gives life to every page. Very special thanks to Margaret Brask, for deciphering dozens of drafts over a five-year period and pulling together a hundred loose ends to facilitate publication.

Our deepest gratitude to family, special friends, and professionals who shaped our content: Mary Smart, Chris Mursau, Doctors Geoff and Leslie Smart, Dr. Price Pritchett, Dr. Robert Perloff, Bruce and Lorelei Bendinger, and so many others too numerous to name. Thank you, thank you!

FOREWORD

Robert Perloff, Ph.D.

MY EARLIER EXPERTISE AS A psychologist specializing in measurement, industrial psychology, consumer behavior, and program evaluation has now coalesced and funneled into that branch of psychology known as "general psychology," which says that I know a bit about many things but not a whole lot about anything in particular. Still, the one fact I know for sure is that Brad Smart and Kate Smart Mursau have poured into this book their combined experience, uncommonly common sense, and jeweled approaches for raising happy and resourceful children.

Smart Parenting is an achievable Rx for cultivating and nurturing kids into fulfilled and successful adults, not to mention into frolicking youngsters making the most of their talents, abilities, and realistic aspirations. *Smart Parenting* is congruent with solid concepts and theories that form the foundation of social and behavioral sciences in general and, I would hasten to guess, child rearing in particular.

Brad and Kate offer a digestible menu of unconditional love, unwavering support, and reinforcing trust, along with uncomplaining patience that parents will use to raise happily fulfilled, can-do kids. They show readers how to model the right behaviors as well, so that their kids will ultimately be equipped to correct their own mistakes. The activies and advice offered by Brad and Kate are not only fitting for parents, grand parents, and other relatives, but also appropriate for supervising personnel at day care centers, as well as for teachers who mentor preschoolers, toddlers, preteens, and adolescents.

I'll wager dollars to doughnuts that the likes of National Public Radio and the early morning wake-up breakfast shows on television and radio will scramble to interview our authors on their proven methods, acquainting program listeners and viewers with this remarkable blueprint for shaping happy and resourceful children.

Dr. Robert Perloff, Distinguished Service Professor Emeritus of Business Administration and of Psychology, Joseph M. Katz Graduate School of Business, University of Pittsburgh.

INTRODUCTION

THE GREATEST GIFT YOU CAN give your children is the motivation and judgment to figure things out for themselves sensibly, every day. Smart Parenting is a groundbreaking approach parents will use with their children to help them become successful in life. It's almost that simple.

We are a father-daughter team that has combined our professional expertise and our own family experiences in developing the methods you will read about in this book. We are both accomplished professionals who want to help parents like you raise your children to be productive in life.

I (Brad) am a management consultant and industrial psychologist for organizations like General Electric, American Heart Association, and others. I am an expert in developing successful people, and have spent over 30 years researching, coaching, and assessing more than 6,000 high achievers, many of whom are among the most gifted people in America. My research, gathered through an extensive interviewing process, has helped me identify the qualities that make people successful, happy, and able or unable to lead balanced, fulfilling lives.

My work demonstrates that most individuals who grew up to

> Smart Parenting is about how parents can help their kids become successful in life.

become happy, successful adults were also resourceful children who never lost their can-do spirit or creativity. But I discovered great discontent among the high-achieving adults I worked with about the children that they themselves were raising. Many of these adults, who felt so successful and confident professionally, did not feel as successful as parents. They felt that they were raising passive, dependent children who floundered when confronted with life's decisions and choices. And in fact, many parents I spoke with didn't consider their children capable of making many smart decisions on their own.

This is not an atypical or unusual concern; in fact, it was also a concern that I discussed with my wife Mary before our own children were born. We decided we would *raise* our children to be resourceful—to retain their natural desire to figure things out for themselves and have the confidence, skills, and judgment to do it.

To do this, we devised specific activities that encouraged resourcefulness and helped them develop the skills they needed to make smart choices and decisions. Although my wife and I often participated in these activities with our children, we frequently didn't tell the kids what to do. Instead, we coached them to figure things out for themselves, in the same way both Kate and I coach our clients.

And the approach worked—the original can-do kids, Kate and her brother Geoff, grew up to be happy in themselves, their marriages, and their careers. Today, Geoff is a successful entrepreneur, active in his community, and the father of three. And Kate, my coauthor, is a practicing clinical psychotherapist who works with children, adults, and families. Her doctoral dissertation focused on resourcefulness in high achievers and their children, and today Kate helps her clients become more independent by showing them how to analyze their problems and figure out solutions. Instead of just giving advice, she tries to help them become more resourceful, so they are more apt and better equipped to solve problems on their own.

In this book, we will give you techniques for teaching your children how to be self-reliant and responsible, an approach that will work with kids at all intellectual levels—from future CEOs to individuals with mental and/or psychological challenges. *Smart Parenting* is based on solid research, utilizing my extensive files on thousands of high achievers and Kate's graduate work and experience in private practice. Kate also vividly remembers how she was coached growing up; she'll tell you what worked and what didn't.

This book reflects our combined insights and experiences and it introduces activities that parents will use to teach their children resourcefulness, activities that are engaging and fun.

The parents with whom we have worked report that even after just one activity they notice improvements in how their children think and act. Their children are able to come up with more ideas and make smarter decisions, and they are more eager to try things on their own. The activities work quickly because they release the creativity, curiosity, and energy kids already have. The tools and parental modeling we teach show kids how to channel their energy and develop the good judgment and decision making that they will use throughout their lives. We know that children really *want* to be highly resourceful. All they need are examples and encouragement. That is the gift this book gives to parents of all types of children.

> Children really *want* to be highly resourceful. All they need are examples and encouragement.

And our method helps parents grow too. Just as I have improved over the years from coaching clients, parents become better and better at coaching their kids as they do the activities. Many parents say *they* become more resourceful and better at making decisions rationally as they perform the activities. While it's true that the activities take time, remember that it's time well spent. After all, what could be a better use of time than bonding with your children while teaching them some of the most important skills in life?

> What could be a better use of time than bonding with your children while teaching them some of the most important skills in life?

As you and your children complete the activities, the benefits of the Smart Parenting approach compound. When children learn to figure things out on their own, they make better decisions and become more confident, responsible, and reliable. This, in turn, leads to even better decision making, greater confidence, and an eagerness to learn and try even more. The activities detailed in this book will start an upward spiral: as you see your children making smarter, more mature decisions, you naturally trust them more and grant them more freedom. They love it—it's truly satisfying because they know they've *earned* their parents' trust and enjoy more independence.

For many parents, the long-term benefits of the Smart Parenting method come when they see their children become happy, successful young adults who make good decisions and achieve their goals in all areas of life. And Smart Parenting isn't just for parents; it's for grandparents, aunts and uncles, other relatives, teachers, and all adults who influence children.

Throughout this book, you will read real-life examples of children who grew up to become the best they could be, with the confidence and passion to pursue their dreams and the drive and skills to achieve them. Perhaps in future editions, some of those examples will be yours, showing how as you used smarter parenting approaches your kids made smarter decisions on their own. Share your experiences with us at our Web site, www.AskSmartParenting.com, which offers ongoing resources to parents like you.

> Smart Parenting isn't just for parents; it's for grandparents, aunts and uncles, other relatives, teachers, and all adults who influence children.

PART ONE

Smart Parenting Building Blocks for Parents

CHAPTER 1

ENJOY THE MAGIC OF SMART PARENTING

Dudley, meanwhile, was counting his presents. His face fell.

"Thirty-six," he said, looking up at his mother and father. "That's two less than last year."

"Darling, you haven't counted Auntie Marge's present, see, it's here under this big one from Mommy and Daddy."

"All right, thirty-seven then," said Dudley, going red in the face. Harry, who could see a huge Dudley tantrum coming on, began wolfing down his bacon as fast as possible in case Dudley turned the table over.

Aunt Petunia obviously sensed danger, too, because she said quickly, "And we'll buy you another two presents while we're out today. How's that, popkin? Two more presents? Is that all right?"

Dudley thought for a moment. It looked like hard work. Finally he said slowly,

"So I'll have thirty…thirty…"

"Thirty-nine, sweetums," said Aunt Petunia.

       —*J.K. Rowling,* Harry Potter and the Sorcerer's Stone[1]

MODERN LIFE CAN BE HARD ON a kid's independence and creativity, particularly if a child, like Dudley, is overindulged and underdisciplined. Most children begin life bursting with curiosity and energy and a passionate desire to explore and figure things out for themselves. (What parent hasn't heard a toddler shout, "I can do it!"?) But how many lose those qualities as they get older?

Many American children spend more than four hours a day sitting passively in front of a television or computer screen—that tells them what to think and do.[2] Between homework and organized activities, unstructured time—time to just play—is shrinking, sometimes to practically nothing, even disappearing from some children's days. Even toddlers don't toddle around the way they once did; strollers are now built to hold children weighing up to 60 pounds. (For some parents, it's easier to push a stroller than to wait for a walking child.) Some studies found the average child doesn't move at all for 80 percent of his or her day. So, it's not surprising that many children lose much of their can-do attitude and the ability to make decisions for themselves because they no longer are given the opportunity.

> The average child doesn't move at all for 80 percent of his or her day.

But kids can rediscover their can-do selves. It's there, lurking below the surface, ready to develop and soar like a butterfly. Do you think that's an exaggeration? It's not; we can show that your child yearns to be resourceful. Ask any child over four years of age who has been to the movies, "What are your favorite movies?" Almost every movie for kids and young adults celebrates resourcefulness. The *Harry Potter* series, the *Home Alone* series, *Finding Nemo*, even *Cinderella*—all feature children (or mice and birds in *Cinderella*) facing challenges and figuring their way out of messes. Adults in the movies sometimes inspire their children's resourcefulness, but mostly the kids are on their own when saving the day. And every child in the movie theater fantasizes about being a hero, a can-do kid. By channeling and guiding your children *now* as they become more resourceful, you will teach judgment and values too.

With the best intentions, adults often play a role in discouraging resourcefulness. Parents want their children to be independent, but they want them to be safe too, so they sometimes overprotect them. For example, they slosh so much sunscreen on their kids that when the children are at a friend's house, they wouldn't consider putting any on. They want their children to succeed, so some over-schedule their kids, give them too much advice, and make too many decisions for them. They want their children to be happy, now, so (like Dudley's parents) they spoil their kids. Rather than teach their child to fix a toy, they buy a new one. Parents may mean well, but they do not always serve their children well.

> Too much advice makes kids passive and dependent on their parents.

Too much advice makes kids passive and dependent on their parents. Both authors see the value of giving their clients *some* advice—and clients ask for it every day. But as a father, I (Brad) saw that too much advice was squelching my children's resourcefulness. So, instead of frequently telling them what to think and do (even when I thought I knew best), I developed activities that encouraged them to be resourceful and taught them how to think for themselves. That's the best antidote I know for society's pressures on parents that drive them to give their kids too much stuff, too much advice, and too much structure.

The Wrong Kind of Ph.D.

Without realizing it, some parents give kids the kind of PHD no one needs.

This PHD stands for all the wrong characteristics: **P**assive, **H**elpless, and **D**ependent.

P is for passive. Passive kids *don't* figure things out—they wait to be told what to do. They don't act or initiate much, except perhaps to ask for yet another purchase. They're spoiled, waiting for parents and other adults to give them things and advice.

H is for helpless. Helpless kids *can't* figure things out. How could they? They've never been taught how—or perhaps have been even discouraged from trying. We all know parents, grandparents, or guardians who either consciously or unconsciously squash a child's initiative with a well-meaning, but ultimately damaging, "Don't touch that—I'll do it!"

D is for dependent. Dependent kids *let* other people figure things out for them and do things for them. They're entirely capable, but have found it easier to let others take care of those issues, chores, and decisions they'd just rather not deal with.

> Too many gifts spoil kids' motivation. Too much advice makes them passive and dependent on you.

The result of P, H, and D is dormant resourcefulness in kids. Too many gifts spoil kids' motivation. Too much advice makes them passive and dependent on you. Parents must come to recognize the mindset behind this lack of resourcefulness and then understand their role in unintentionally encouraging that mindset.

Being passive, helpless, and dependent—like Dudley in *Harry Potter*—is a dangerous way to go through life. Sometimes, adults send mixed messages to kids. We may allow them to choose hobbies or activities (soccer or piano), but seldom allow them to initiate, organize, or create after-school activities for themselves. We encourage them to be physically active, and some serious athletes are, but most kids get exercise for only a few hours a week, usually during sports or classes supervised and organized by adults. Certainly we give them plenty of opportunities to think about what they will buy (with money we give them!), but not much practice managing a budget, solving their own problems, or formulating and expressing thoughts about the world around them or about moral values.

It's ironic that today's youth enjoy unprecedented opportunities for accomplishment, but many lack the tools—whether initiative, drive, or intellectual maturity—to become resilient, resourceful, and self-reliant. It seems as though people in past generations were motivated by the challenges of their youth; they seemed to thrive and grow by dealing with adversity. In contrast, many children today have nothing like the kind of freedom, independence, and responsibility with which kids developed in the past. Is it surprising that kids who never had the chance to organize a sandlot baseball game or figure out how to build a go-cart or fix a tractor show little initiative?

As a society we *say* we want our kids to show initiative, to be creative, to be responsible, and to use good judgment. Unfortunately, we don't give them the opportunities to develop these qualities. Toys R Us™ stores have entire sections devoted to stimulating creativity, but most of the toys involve making crafts, and almost none stimulate creativity in resolving conflicts, avoiding drugs, or starting a lawn-mowing business.

With the wonders of technology and innovation, adults are able to give the children in their charge the latest in entertainment and education. In general, parents offer children too many pre-packaged, pre-organized experiences that almost encourage passivity. Too much television and Internet and too many videos and repetitive electronic games can foster seclusion and introverted behavior. We allow our kids to consume too much of their free time in passive video viewing or violent and repetitive video games of questionable moral value.

Conversely, parents are overly involved when they too often say, "Let me do that for you" or "Let me show you." They are trying to be helpful, and usually are—but not always. Parents must show how to change a light bulb safely, for example, but too often parents do things kids could do or give advice just to save time. Whatever the intention, too much advice sends the message: "You can't do it, so I'll do it" or "The way you will do it won't be good enough, so follow my instruction." A child will eventually conclude, "I can't do anything on my own," "I'm not competent," "I'm not worthy." PHD is the most powerful self-esteem squasher on earth. Enemies of the United States of America could only wish for an entire generation of Americans possessing that self-defeating PHD.

> When we overprotect children, we're sending a message, "You can't take care of things yourself."

Similarly, when we overprotect children, we're sending a message, "You can't take care of things yourself." There is a difference between prudent protection and overprotection. We all know the world can be dangerous. It's not being overprotective to walk or drive your nine-year-old to school, if you live in a city or even some suburbs. It's understandable when parents brush their five-year-old's teeth, but wouldn't it be better to teach the child to do it?

Even with all the pressures on kids and parents today, it's possible to raise children who will grow up to be happy, successful adults—adults who can act with resourcefulness and confidence in an uncertain world. How can parents do that? Through the power of positive parenting, that's how.

The Power of Positive Parenting

The first step in Smart Parenting may seem obvious: for sure, avoid negative parenting. But you know that!

Negative parenting has many aspects: physical and mental abuse, extreme neglect, constant criticism, and belittling. Naturally, children who are treated in any of these ways are going to feel they're not worth much. The greater the degree to which a child feels worthless, the worse he or she will behave; and if the child's behavior makes parents react even more negatively, the whole family becomes caught in a downward spiral.

For sure, avoid negative parenting.

Children from families like this rarely develop all aspects of themselves and their talents so their efforts to become happy, successful adults are stunted. Of course, some people do manage to triumph over horrible childhoods, but the odds of doing this completely and without psychological damage are not good. The sad fact is that many people from troubled families carry emotional baggage for the rest of their lives, baggage that makes it difficult for them to be happy in important aspects of their lives, whether in business, in personal relationships, or as parents themselves. For example, they may achieve career success, but fail at marriage, or they may become very negative parents themselves. After all, that's all they know.

Since you're reading this book, or any book on parenting, it's clear that you take your responsibilities seriously and you have good intentions to practice positive parenting. You want to be a positive parent. In many ways, you probably already are—or at least that's your intention. (Negative parents wouldn't be reading this!)

Positive parenting means that you are constantly giving your children love, respect, and praise. Positive parents keep their children safe—physically and emotionally. Positive parents model and teach good behavior and beliefs. Positive parents encourage self-confidence and a host of other positive feelings in their children, such as happiness, trust, the ability to feel and show affection, and pride in accomplishment. This is the kind of behavior in children that creates and inspires an *upward* spiral of more positive parenting.

Unfortunately, positive parenting alone isn't enough to raise resourceful kids.

Many parents who provide this type of parenting still might thwart self-reliance in their children by overprotecting, overstructuring, overadvising, and overindulging

> **Positive parenting alone isn't enough.**

them. The abusive parent threatens and criticizes a child into submission, whereas the loving but overprotective parent can smother a child in a protective cocoon and remove opportunities for accomplishment, though with the best of intentions. In neither case will a child ever reach full potential because he or she simply lacks the resourcefulness to do so.

Kate's doctoral dissertation on the success of high achievers found resourcefulness to be the most important of dozens of skills. In fact, 95 percent of career high achievers considered resourcefulness to be either extremely important or very important to their career success. Yet, ironically, most of them inadvertently prevented their own children from becoming resourceful.

I (Kate) asked the high achievers to rate their children's resourcefulness and then provide examples. When independent psychologists evaluated the responses, almost without exception they found the children to be far less resourceful than their successful parents thought they were. In a preliminary study, I

> **High achievers found resourcefulness to be the most important of dozens of skills.**

surveyed 3,000 ordinary parents, asking for examples of resourcefulness in their children. Less than 5 percent of parents could think of even one example of resourcefulness in their children.

Over the years, the thousands of high achievers that Brad interviewed told him that they had been successful because they were highly resourceful, but lamented that they'd inadvertently stifled resourcefulness in their children. This concern that we both shared led us to write this book and provide insights that every parent can use.

The Smart Parenting Equation

Resourceful children and adults begin each day energized—they're not just *able* to deal with whatever the day brings, but also eager to do it. They live with zest. They *love* figuring out how to get over, around, or through barriers to success. Resourcefulness is motivation (drive, energy, and passion) guided by the ability to make good, rational decisions. That's the Smart Parenting equation—and it requires both motivation *and* good decision-making skills.

> ### Smart Parenting Equation
> **Resourcefulness = Motivation x Decision Making**

Children who are bursting with energy, confidence, and creativity can make disastrous decisions with terrible consequences if they don't learn how to think things through. On the other hand, having good, sensible judgment but no passion, no spark, or no energy is awful too. Lack of motivation prevents creativity and denies the child deep joy and satisfaction. The Smart Parenting Model depicted in Figure 1-1 will give you a general overview of various parenting styles and their typical results.

Smart Parenting Takes Time

Initially, being the kind of parent who rears resourceful children takes more time. Yes, Smart Parenting involves positive behavior, but it's much more than that. You need to know your children—*really* know them—and that takes time. It takes longer to ask a child questions and

Parent Behaviors	Child's Feelings, Beliefs	Child's Behaviors	Predicted Adult Life
Negative Behaviors			
Neglects, abuses, stifles kids; is hyper-critical, impatient, dishonest; gives little praise; discipline is non-existent or harsh.	"I'm not okay," "I'm not worthy," "People are threatening," "I'm a victim," "That makes me mad!" or "I'm a bad person."	Has few if any goals; lazy; blames others; could act out, throw tantrums, is hostile; unrealistic.	Adult carries serious emotional baggage, has low self-esteem, rarely achieves success in most aspects of life; depression or even suicide are possible.
Positive Behaviors Without Smart Parenting			
Shows kids love, respect, support; spends quality time together; praises and provides safety; disciplines.	"I'm okay, but not great," "I deserve things without work-ing hard or setting high goals," "The world is not threa-tening and I'm safe."	Has realistically modest goals; may whine, sulk; may be hard to discipline.	Underachiever; does not solve diffi-cult problems in career, relationship, and most aspects of life.
Positive Behaviors Can Be Nullified By:			
Overprotects, over-structures, and spoils children, which squelches resourcefulness.	"I can't do it," "I give up," "Can I have some money?" "What should I do?"	Has low goals; passive, helpless, dependent on others (has "PHD").	Adult may be moderately happy, but likely to be an underachiever or a conscientious plodder; even if very intelligent, may shy away from decisions that could increase happiness.
Smart Parenting With Positive Behaviors			
Builds resourceful-ness by encouraging independence, coaching child to solve problems and make wise decisions in all aspects of life.	"No, don't tell me—I can figure it out," "This is fun!" "It's hard but I bet I can do it," "Let me try!" "Life is great!"	Sets high goals; realistic view of self and the world; confident leader; has real zest for life, resilient, can-do attitude.	Adult has drive, energy, passion; is happy and success-ful in most ways; high self-esteem; eager to take on whatever life brings; can handle most challenges and will always try.

Figure 1-1. The Smart Parenting Model

wait for answers or to coach kids through learning than to simply tell them what to do. However, it will be time well spent. Through Smart Parenting you will be connecting with your children in a much more meaningful way as you teach them important skills for becoming the kind of adults you want them to eventually be.

One regretful parent told me, "I should have put in the time when the children were young doing the things that prevent problems, because now I'm putting in more time and money trying to fix the kids' problems."

There is no getting around the fact that being a great parent does take time. You may not spend a *lot* more time than you did when you were being solely a positive parent, but you will probably spend it much differently with Smart Parenting. Sometimes parents will work with their children jointly, but many times it will be one on one. You may also have to put your children's needs higher on your daily priority list. Children's feelings and needs can't be scheduled; they want to talk when they're in the mood to talk or something happens that they want to talk about. They need you when they need you, and you can't determine when that will be. You need to be on call for when they want to give you a hug, or get your help, or just know that you're there in the background *if* they need you.

> **There is no getting around the fact that being a great parent does take time.**

If this sounds overwhelming, take heart. There is a wonderfully, bright, time-saving light at the end of the Smart Parenting journey: Smart Parenting eventually requires less time "parenting!"

MarineMax CEO Bill McGill relates that his very strict parents encouraged him to be resourceful, so much so that after his sophomore year in high school, he was granted almost 100 percent independence— no curfews, very little advice except when he asked for it, and hardly any admonitions. Since then, he and his parents have related to each other as friends. His parents no longer had to *allocate* time to "parenting" because Bill had become such a resourceful, responsible young adult.

> **Smart Parenting eventually requires less time "parenting!"**

We hope that you can arrange your life so that, between the two of you parents or, if you're a single parent, between you and a support network, your children get the time and attention they need when they need it. You should also know that we've designed our advice to meet the realities of being a parent and a working adult in the twenty-first century. The approach and activities in this book all assume that your time with your children is more limited than you'd like it to be. We know that your day can be long and making a living also has to be a high priority. We want you to know that we respect your time and your children's time, and we've tried to make good use of it—for all of you.

All children and parents are unique, but parents who have tried the Smart Parenting activities offer some useful generalizations and tips, which we as professionals support and have adapted for this book. The 11 Smart Parenting tips below deliver field-tested guidance for how to make the activities throughout this book successful. We suggest that you read them now before reading the activities, and reread them periodically as you try activities.

11 Smart Parenting Tips

1. **When you brainstorm ideas, keep going until *your child* comes up with an idea he or she is really excited about.** When you are doing an activity, there will be goals to set and lots of decisions to make. Fight the temptation to take over. Draw ideas out of your child. Usually your attention, support, and questions will ignite your child's imagination and you will both be excited by how many ideas your child creates. If this doesn't happen, don't get defensive or show disappointment.

2. **Modify an idea or activity if the original is too ambitious for the available time and attention needed.** For example, building a wooden platform with sides is a more realistic Saturday project than a Swiss Family Robinson-style tree house.

3. **Allow enough time for the activity and let your child set the pace.** Plan plenty of extra time for an activity, so you can both relax and the child has time to ask questions, express opinions, and succeed mostly on his or her own—even if making lots

of mistakes along the way. Let your child set the pace: you'll both have more fun, and your child will learn more.

4. **Be patient.** Most successful people are very goal-oriented. You will probably see many more effective ways to complete the task at hand than your child will. Remind yourself frequently that the goal is for your child to develop decision-making and problem-solving skills and become more resourceful, not to build the best tree house on the planet in record time.

5. **Ask questions to help the child figure things out.** Don't make many suggestions, limit expressing your opinions, and don't give more than 10 percent of the answers. If your child gets stuck, you can ask leading questions or give hints.

6. **Listen actively.** Don't do more than 10 percent of the talking. Sometimes what is interesting to children can be boring to adults, especially busy parents. Relax and try to understand what your child is saying anyway—when you don't listen, you're sending the message that your child is not worth listening to! Besides, if you really listen, you may learn something new about your child.

7. **Provide safety nets, but don't be overprotective.** Refusing to allow 10-year-olds to hammer nails because they might bang their fingers is being overprotective. Climbing an old ladder first yourself to make sure it's safe is sensible.

8. **Be a cheerleader: praise, praise, praise your child whenever he or she figures something out or does something on his or her own.** Show your child how great you think that is. The more specific the praise, the better. Be sure your methods of praise come across as sincere and are appreciated by your child. You'll know you've done it right when you give praise and your child beams with pride. Many great parents say, "Good for you—you figured it out on your own!" They give high fives, literally cheer, and brag to other adults. Whatever works!

> **Be a cheerleader. Praise, praise, praise your child!**

9. **Show faith in your child.** Feel and communicate your belief that your child can succeed. Jack Welch, retired CEO of General Electric and one of Brad's clients, said his mother contributed most to his success and was his biggest cheerleader. "I *know* you can do it, Jack," she'd say at the beginning of every endeavor.

10. **Convey nonstop, unconditional love and total respect for your child, all the time.** No exceptions. None.

11. **Accept backsliding and occasional failures.** Treat mistakes for what they are: valuable learning opportunities. Life is more a series of obstacles than successes. Children who believe they should never risk failure become children who are afraid to try. If your child builds a toy glider and it doesn't fly, find something to praise sincerely: "You learned something new today: that the 24-hour glue really does have to set for 24 hours. Good for you for trying—and now you know how to make it more flyable next time!"

Remember that the short-term goal is to have fun together and help your child become more confident and resourceful. If the child performs perfectly, learns a new skill, or makes something beautiful, that's an added bonus, but it's not the goal. Fun is essential in motivating the child to actually do the activities. Fun stimulates and increases that passion and zest for life. Fun is the high-octane fuel for resourcefulness. Let your child do the thinking and make the decisions; the long-term goal is to raise a can-do kid who grows up to create a happy, fulfilling life.

> **Fun is the high-octane fuel for resourcefulness.**

How much help to give along the way is an important judgment call. As you go through each activity, you will use your knowledge of your child to decide when and how much to:

- Actively coach and praise your child, make suggestions, or even cancel the activity.
- Actively back away. If, for example, your child is making decisions well and is self-motivated, you won't need to intervene—your role will be simply to praise your child and enjoy hanging out.

Ultimately you are preparing your children to be able to do *everything* by themselves, because that's what they'll do when they grow up and leave home. You are preparing them for that by encouraging them to be passionate about life and to make intelligent decisions.

We expect that, when you start using this book, you will formally do a couple of activities each week with your children. Later on, you will probably find yourself doing less as your children take on more. Instead of formally doing Smart Parenting activities, you will encourage resourcefulness with a nod, a question, or a smile. Over time your children will become increasingly resourceful and independent and, like Bill McGill's parents, you will revel in the emergence of your can-do kids.

Notes

1. Rowling, J.K., *Harry Potter and the Sorcerer's Stone*. New York: Scholastic Press, 1997.

2. American Academy of Child and Adolescent Psychiatry.

CHAPTER 2

COACH YOUR CHILD TO BECOME A GREAT DECISION MAKER

Jennifer grinned ear to ear. In her seven years of life, she hadn't done anything like this—start a business. This morning her mom asked her if she would like to try one of those resourcefulness activities and Jennifer replied, "Sure, I'd like to open a lemonade stand and you and Megan (her little sister) can be my helpers." Jennifer chose the location, designed the stand, purchased lemons and sugar cheap (from her mom), trained her sister to pour and collect money, and delegated work (like fetching a table) to her mom. An hour later, Jennifer was ready for business. Her mom followed Smart Parenting principles and simply coached Jennifer to make her own decisions, keeping advice to a minimum and checking on her daughters periodically during the day. At 3 p.m. Jennifer came running in and exclaimed, "We made $20 and here's your $5 for stuff, so we keep $15! Waddya think, Mom?"

That afternoon Jennifer's mom, while out running errands, couldn't stop thinking about her first Smart Parenting activity—how strange the morning was, yet how wonderful. As manager of a large department at work, she was accustomed to giving advice and directions.

At home she usually did the same thing with Jennifer: "Clean up your room," "Don't forget your soccer uniform," "Apologize or you'll lose a friend," "Here, let me do that math problem for you." Following Smart Parenting guidelines, this morning she mostly hung out with Jennifer, joking, having fun, and gently asking questions like "Fifty cents is expensive—what do you think?" and "What are possible locations for the lemonade stand?" and "Are there any disadvantages in using expensive, real lemons?"

That night as she was tucking Jennifer into bed, her daughter gave her a big hug and kiss and said, "Today was cool, Mom. I like figuring things out with you as my helper. I like it a lot!" And her mom thought, "It's wonderful seeing Jennifer become a can-do kid!"

—From a proud Smart Parent

WHEN YOU SHOW CHILDREN HOW TO make everyday decisions rationally and help them practice doing it, they will have the necessary skills when trying to reach an important goal or deciding about something that really matters. Nearly all of the activities in this book help children practice decision making and problem solving. In this chapter, we will help you set the example of a rational decision maker and demonstrate how to coach your children to be one.

> People who make decisions rationally—who analyze a situation, set a goal, consider the options, and then systematically decide what to do—have an enormous advantage in life.

People who make decisions rationally—who analyze a situation, set a goal, consider the options, and then systematically decide what to do—have an enormous advantage in life. If this doesn't sound like you, don't worry! Another advantage of doing the activities is that your own decision-making skills will improve too.

There are many ways to effectively solve problems and make rational decisions; if you have a process that works for you, teach it to your children. Bill McGill, whom we introduced in the previous chapter as the CEO of MarineMax, the largest boat dealership corporation in the world, shared with us the way his father taught him to solve problems:

> If I was stymied, I'd ask my dad for help, and instead of giving me answers, he'd start asking a lot of questions. He instinctively knew it would be better for me if I figured things out, rather than having him simply fix the bailing machine or whatever. If there was a problem on the lift system, he'd ask what I thought the different solutions might be. We'd sometimes go take a look, and he'd ask me if I might be overlooking something. He would ask me what I saw happening here, and what the different causes could be. After awhile I learned to just ask myself the same kinds of questions, and in a sense I learned the same sort of decision-making approaches I now use as the head of a public corporation!

If you don't have a decision-making model, following are two you can use. Ann Drake, CEO of DSC Logistics, still uses the method her father taught her. Whenever she asked him what she should do, he'd say, "Use the decision model!" (Figure 2-1 on next page.) When, for example, she wanted a bike, she got a piece of paper, wrote down her choices (wait for birthday, borrow cousin's bike, earn the money and buy own bike), and then listed the advantages and disadvantages of each. Ann says:

> Dad didn't set my goals for me or tell me which option to pick. Even when I was a little girl he might ask, "Can you think of any other options?" and sometimes suggest something I hadn't considered or add an advantage or disadvantage based on his experience as an adult. But the main thing was he taught me to believe in my ability to carefully figure things out myself.

The Smarts used a slightly more complex decision-making approach to clarify the goal, think of options to get there, and then execute those options. We call it the SMART Decision Pad. It was never a rigid process. Sometimes going through all of the steps would have been too cumbersome. The order of the steps changed depending on the situation. Sometimes stating the situation came first, sometimes clarifying the goal came first, and sometimes it took a lot of talking to understand what the goal was. But all the basic steps were taught. Discussing each step when it's appropriate is a good way to teach children the full decision-making process, as well as about the value of having goals and how to consider consequences.

	ANN DRAKE'S DECISION MODEL
	My Goal: Get a Bike

OPTION 1: BORROW COUSIN'S BIKE

Advantages	Disadvantages
Usually his bike is available.	& but not always!
Can still get new bike for my birthday.	It's a boy's bike!

OPTION 2: WAIT FOR MY BIRTHDAY

Get my own bike.	Waiting—my birthday is in 6 months.

OPTION 3: EARN MONEY TO BUY BIKE

Get exactly the bike I want.	Would take all summer.
Work could be fun.	Work might not be fun.
Feel good about being independent.	

Figure 2-1. Ann Drake's decision model

The SMART Decision Pad

Below we've broken the process down into five steps to make it easier to learn and put into daily practice.

The SMART Decision Pad

1. **S** Study the *situation*.

2. **M** Make the *goal* clear.

3. **A** Assess various *options*.

4. **R** Realize the *best option* and do it.

5. **T** Take stock: *evaluate* how the SMART process worked.

Let's walk through each step.

1. S—Study the *situation*. Ask questions to help put the situation, problem, or opportunity into the child's own words. Do *not* assume that you know what's going on (even if you really do) and don't speak for your child. Putting whatever is going on into *his* own words will help him think about the issue clearly. Wait for him to describe the situation, or help him do that with neutral questions like "What happened?" Clarify the situation; get your child to tell you what really happened in detail, and then ask how and why it happened. Ask follow-up questions such as "What did she say then?" or "How do you know?" or "Why do you think that happened?" to help your child understand the situation better and get some distance from it, too.

2. M—Make the *goal* clear. What's the goal? Ask questions that will put the goal into words—even if the goal seems obvious. You as a parent can help your child set a clear goal with questions like "What would make you happy?" or "How would you like to see this turn out?" Sometimes you'll need to dwell on Step 1 (study the situation) quite a while before you can identify the goal.

For example, Jae, a friend's daughter, complained that she hated taking the bus to school. She said her goal was for her mother to drive her. But as they went through Step 1 it become obvious that her *real* goal was to get the bus bully to stop picking on her and then (if she could) to stop feeling afraid of him.

3. A—Assess various *options*. Brainstorm ideas for what can be done to reach the goal. In brainstorming, you think of as many ideas as possible. Tell your child that even silly, inappropriate ideas are just fine when you're brainstorming. She can pick the best one later. (This is because the more relaxed and uncritical you are, the easier it is for her to think of many various possibilities.) You can accomplish this through questions, too: "What can you do about it?" Or, for older children, "What are your options?" Keep asking until you sense your child has really thought of everything she can. In the bus situation, Jae thought of eleven options (Figure 2-2).

List the pros and cons of each option. Ask questions like "What do you think would happen if you …?," "How would you feel then?," "What would be good about that?," and "What would be bad?" Do *not* judge the ideas. Try to ask neutral questions that force your child to consider the consequences. ("What do you think Jimmy would do if you punched him? What would the other children think? How would you feel?") Neutral questions enable most children to make the appropriate judgment call themselves.

SMART Decision Pad	
Jae's Goal: Not be picked on by bus bully	
OPTION 1: MOM DRIVES ME	
Advantages	**Disadvantages**
Not picked on when in car.	Could still be picked on by some bully at school.
OPTION 2: TELL BULLY TO STOP	
Quick (tomorrow).	Probably not work.
OPTION 3: PUNCH BULLY	
Might work.	Might get me hurt and punished.
OPTION 4: TAKE KARATE LESSONS	
Might work; feel I can defend myself when need to.	Might get me hurt and punished.
OPTION 5: FIGHT BACK VERBALLY	
Nonviolent solution.	Bully might just laugh and keep bullying. I might not be able to think of anything to say.
OPTION 6: THROW RAW EGG	
Get even.	Get punished.
OPTION 7: ASK OTHER KIDS' IDEAS	
Possibly get good ideas.	Possibly not get good ideas.

Figure 2-2. Eleven options for dealing with the bus bully (continued on next page)

SMART Decision Pad	
Jae's Goal: Not be picked on by bus bully	
OPTION 8: TELL TEACHER	
Advantages	**Disadvantages**
Get bully in trouble.	Kids call me tattle tale and bully might hit me.
OPTION 9: ROLE PLAY VERBAL REBUFFS	
Build confidence to at least talk back.	Take weeks to build confidence.
OPTION 10: IGNORE BULLY	
Bully loses interest and stops.	Bully gets more angry and threatening.
OPTION 11: DO # 4, 7, AND 9	
Best chance of success, can defend myself and have allies.	Would take time. Threatening.

Figure 2-2. Eleven options for dealing with the bus bully (continued)

4. R—Realize the *best option* and do it! When all the options are laid out on the SMART Decision Pad, the best one usually stands out. Encourage your child to make the final decision. Then watch her act on it. If she hesitates, ask, "When will you do it?" The "it"—her decision—might be to talk to a friend she had ignored, cancel a movie in order to study for a test, or tell a boyfriend she won't go out with him if he continues using illegal drugs. Doing it is the toughest part of the process. Praise the child for completing the process—"You've done a great job thinking it all through!"—and let her get started. If it feels right, you can also ask if there is anything your child would like you to help with; if there isn't, say something encouraging and leave it at that. "You've made a really good plan—I'm proud of you. Good luck tomorrow! I'll be interested in hearing how it goes." Be a cheerleader for your child.

5. T—Take stock: *evaluate* how the SMART Decision Pad process worked. The final step is to discuss what worked, what didn't and why, and what your child would do differently if the situation occurred again or what he would do the same way. If nothing worked, encourage him to keep trying. Be a role model for persistence: ask questions about what to do next, and help your child think of new ideas to try.

In the case of the bully and his sidekicks on the bus, role-playing with her mother helped a little, but Jae decided to take karate lessons anyway: "So I won't feel scared." Eventually, through a combination of confronting the bully and sticking up for herself, making friends with some of the other children and getting them on her side, and knowing that if it came to a fight she'd have a good chance of winning, the bully stopped bullying. And Jae stopped being afraid to go on the bus.

The SMART Decision Pad is a handy tool, but it's not necessary to use it for every decision. Many parents say their child uses it three or four times each week, after he or she gets the hang of it. You can teach your child the individual steps by creating mini-activities.

For example, brainstorming is such an important part of the decision-making model, and so much fun, that we urge you to do it on the fly, often! Ask kids to figure out solutions to everyday dilemmas. For example, you could say, "Hmm, we're all out of detergent and I need to wash these clothes right now. Got any ideas?" If they say, "Go to the store." You say, "Yes, that's one option." Make a game of it, "What else could I do? See how many things you can think of—we can pick the best idea when we have four or five to choose from." Be upbeat and encourage your kids to think of more and more ideas, just the way you would if you were brainstorming at work and trying to loosen everyone up to think of really creative solutions to a tough problem. Remember that in the brainstorming phase no idea is too silly and no idea is too small—you're thinking creatively.

> Be upbeat and encourage your kids to think of more and more ideas.

You want your children's minds to be as free and open as they can be. The way to open them is by being encouraging and giving sincere praise. Meaningless, false praise does not do anything for your child. However, if a child who's normally passive and dependent on you for ideas starts coming up with ideas of his own, by all means, show your pride and excitement: "Those are six original creative ideas! Good for you!"

Showing your children that you have reasons behind *your own* decisions is another good way to teach them how to make decisions rationally and methodically. Growing up, I (Kate) remember that my parents occasionally imposed decisions on me, but they *always* explained why. They'd say things like "No, we don't think you should spend the night at Alison's, because you have a big presentation tomorrow and you need a good night's sleep." As a child, it always surprised me when my friends' parents would say, "Just because." In our family, my parents purposely thought out loud in front of us, so we could see how adults made decisions. Examples can be powerful teaching tools—particularly if you can resist the temptation to lecture and preach.

But examples alone aren't enough; kids need practice. The SMART Decision Pad process has five steps that you can inch into gradually. Coach your child through the process of making rational decisions in a logical way by beginning with small, everyday decisions.

For example, suppose your child says, "For Mom's birthday, I made a present—but I'd like to do something that's a surprise too." Instead of offering a suggestion, ask what your child would like to do and listen to her answer, offering praise or another question: "That's a good idea! What else do you have in mind?"

Eventually, after you've coached your child through smaller, everyday decisions— and most of the activities in this book give plenty of opportunities to do that—you could try using the complete SMART Decision Pad to make a more important decision or solve a big problem. My father (Brad) taught it to me when I was 13 years old to make a hard choice. I had always loved softball and got to be pretty good at the sport, until one year when tryouts warned of a looming problem.

> The SMART Decision Pad process has five steps that you can inch into gradually.

I remember having mono and strep throat at the time of tryouts and struggling with fatigue. I was missing easy pitches when I was at bat, as if my aim was slightly off. Despite these problems, I made the team and was excited to play, but I also worried about how tired and sluggish I was all the time. It seemed that I was always tired. Even dinner was exhausting.

I just wanted to go to sleep as my father asked about the daily news and quizzed me on various world leaders. I got so frustrated and irritable that one night during dinner I broke down and cried. My mother cried too; later she said it was because she was happy that I finally was opening up, but sad I was in so much pain. My father asked me if I wanted to come into his office after dinner to figure out what was causing me to be so upset. So, after dinner I grabbed a Diet Pepsi™ and shuffled in.

First he asked me to list all the activities I was part of. As I talked, he wrote down everything I said. He listed all the activities on the right side and then asked me how much time each one took. No wonder I was exhausted. When we added it all up, I realized that I had *no* free time and only slept for 6.5 hours—and sometimes even less! Then my father asked me to list my activities in terms of priority: "What things are a must? What's lower on the totem pole?" he asked. After I'd gone through everything else, my dad pushed on: "How do you feel about softball?" I had been dreading being asked that question. It was as if he was asking it in slow motion. "My team needs me ... and I need the team. I love the competition, I love the sport, my coach, my team-mates, and it gives me a break during the day."

"It all sounds great and wonderful," my dad said. "I think I understand the pros of softball. What are the cons to playing this season?" Hesitantly, I said, "It takes a lot of hours during the day." "Ten hours plus for the week," he said. Then, I admitted that I was struggling, "And I don't have much energy. I'm not performing well, and I am getting stressed out because I need more time for homework and I'm not getting enough sleep." Until then, I hadn't realized that there were so many cons and that it was affecting my physical and emotional well-being so much.

My dad homed in on the issue, asking, "What would be the advantages or disadvantages of taking a season off from softball—just one season?" For me the disadvantages would be abandoning my goal of being on varsity all year round, losing out on the "team" component that I loved, not getting much exercise, and missing out on all the fun that came with playing the game. Advantages were that it would allow me more time to do homework, which would improve my grades, and I would not be so stressed. I would get more sleep, which would probably give me more energy. My health would probably improve and my mood would improve too as a result.

After I went through all the pros and cons, I concluded that it would be in my best interest to give up softball for the season. My dad said he was very proud of me and that he thought I was making the right decision; he didn't care what I dropped, as long as I achieved a better balance. After doing the activity with my dad, I began to feel much better—I could even feel the tension in my neck start to ease.

SMART Decision Pad	
Kate's Goal: 10 more hours per week for studies and sleep	
OPTION 1: DROP ZAMBIAN EXCHANGE CLUB	
Advantages	Disadvantages
Free up 2 hours.	Lose credibility with members since I am founder and president.
OPTION 2: DROP A CLASS	
Free up 5 hours.	Would have to take summer class.
OPTION 3: DROP ACTIVITIES WHERE I'M ONLY A MEMBER (SADD, ENVIRONMENTAL CLUB)	
Free up 2 hours.	Less overall time with members.
Not very involved.	Feel guilty.
OPTION 4: DROP VARSITY SOFTBALL 1 SEASON	
Free up 10-15 hours.	Miss excitement of competition.
Alternative would be dropping more than 1 activity.	Less exercise.

Figure 2-3. Kate's decision pad

I grew up a bit after learning what we now call the SMART Decision Pad process. To this day, whenever I have a conflict or dilemma, I start by analyzing the situation and figuring out what I really want—my goal. Then I list the possible solutions and the pros and cons of each. This enables me to think through all the alternatives. Ultimately

I'm usually happy and confident in my solution. I think this skill has helped me in life and even in my career choice as a psychotherapist because I teach my clients the exact same approach. In counseling or therapy, I help people identify what their problems are and how *they* can solve them. I try not to tell people what to do, but instead I help them figure it out.

In retrospect, my dad had concluded I should give up softball, but at the time I felt it was *my* decision. He had confidence that the SMART Decision Pad would work for me and it did.

While this worked for me, we had already been practicing some Smart Parenting activities with smaller problems for quite some time. But this was the first time we used the full SMART Decision Pad. It's important to know when your child is ready to make such a big decision and how much help from you is appropriate. It's also important to know when you as a parent should simply make the decision, rather than using the model at all. There are times when you really do know best and when the stakes are so high you can't risk the consequences of your child making a wrong decision.

> There are times when you really do know best and when the stakes are so high you can't risk the consequences of your child making a wrong decision.

One particular example comes to mind. The daughter of one parent we know, Erin, entered a new school that was much bigger than her old one. She was shy; she missed her old friends and hadn't yet made new ones. She was good at soccer, and her parents thought being on the team would help her get to know the other kids. They also knew that tryouts were being held and that Erin hadn't signed up. Her father decided that this would be a good time to use the SMART Decision Pad model we had given him—but he didn't really let Erin make the decision. He said things like "It seems to me that the problem is shyness, the goal is to make some friends, and since you're such a good soccer player, the best option is to try out for the team, right?" and Erin, feeling more and more manipulated, finally exploded, "Why don't you just *order* me to join the team?"

Actually, in this case, that might have been better. Sometimes parents *do* know better than children and in this situation, since her father was sure he knew what was best and was going to steer Erin toward the outcome he wanted whatever she said, it would have been better if he had given a straightforward directive: "Erin, I moved a lot as a kid, so I know what it's like, and I know what worked (and what didn't work) for me. I'm going to make this decision for you because I can't stand to see you miss this chance. It won't come again until next year and I'm afraid you'd really regret not trying out. And I'm *sure* that if you try out you'll make the team and that will help you get to know the other kids and make friends. You've always made friends through being on teams! *Please* try out for soccer. If you want to quit after two weeks, I promise I won't say a thing. Just trust me for two weeks—if I'm wrong, tell me so and quit."

Erin did not quit and two months later was outgoing, had friends, and once again was a can-do kid. Forcing a decision on her might have given her the dreaded PHD, but it didn't. You must judge which risk is worth taking: whether to allow your child to make what you know is a bad decision or impose your own solution and risk making your child more dependent on you.

We believe that when you really do know better than your child and the stakes are high—that is, when making the wrong choice could really hurt your child—you *should* make the decision. It's your responsibility as a parent. When you do make a decision for your child, explain your reasoning and listen to your child's reaction, but be honest about whose decision it is.

Coaching your child to make good decisions is not something to always be scheduled ("Today we're going to learn to use the SMART Decision Pad"), but something you can slip into everyday situations and conversations. We recommend doing it informally and frequently. Older children will appreciate your nonjudgmental questions, coaching, and encouragement; younger ones will

> Coaching your child to make good decisions is not something to always be scheduled, but something you can slip into everyday situations and conversations.

delight in solving simple problems for themselves. Even two-year-olds can get started—with your help of course!

I (Brad) am now encouraging my grandchildren. Three-year-old Will couldn't unlock a gate, but wanted the ball that had landed on the other side of the fence. I said, "Oh no, the gate's locked. But I bet you can figure out another way to get the ball. I can think of a way. Can you?" Will thought hard—I could almost see his brain working. Suddenly he ran, got a stool, and climbed over the gate and dropped to the ground, grinning. He threw the ball back, proudly; I caught it and praised him for getting it: "You did that all by yourself and you figured it out all by yourself—that's great! You're really good at figuring things out!" Will beamed, but then looked serious. "Pops, would you please gimme the stool so I can get back over the fence?"

What Smart Parenting Looks Like Most Days

If you watched a DVD of Smart Parenting techniques in action, what would you see? Eighty percent of the time parents are doing no more than letting their children do things for themselves, 15 percent of the time they gently coach their children using some version of the SMART Decision Pad, and 5 percent of the time parents will be practicing one of the resourcefulness activities described in this book. Extremely busy parents do a lot for their kids just to get them to school on time, not miss soccer practice, or help them finish homework and get to bed. But those parents who are committed to building their children's resourcefulness steadily—day after day and month after month—mold their kids into becoming independent (Figure 2-4).

On a daily basis, smart parents can do more than patiently restrain their inclination to jump in and take over. Instead, they can create "teaching moments"—priceless opportunities to invest in their children's resourcefulness. In most cases, it's better to teach your child *how* to think, not *what* to think.

> **Teach your child *how* to think, not *what* to think.**

Suppose you and your 10-year-old Heather are hiking and need to get across a creek, eight feet wide and a foot deep. Heather is about to

Smart Parenting Opportunity ...	Missed ...	Taken ...
Toddler who can put on her shoes	Parent does it for her	Parent encourages toddler to do it
Seven-year-old should leave for soccer practice now, but his bike tire needs air	Parent pumps up tire or drives him to practice	Parent suggests child pump up tire
Ten-year-old has fight with best friend	Parent calls friend's parent to resolve the problem	Parent coaches child to figure out positive solution
15-year-old's project is missing a one-paragraph summary; it's 11 p.m.	Parent writes it	Parent does not offer to "rescue" child, but instead asks, "What are your key points?"

Figure 2-4. Smart parenting opportunities

wade in. For the past few months, you (her mom) have been nurturing her resourcefulness, and Heather has become more of a can-do kid, but she's about to get very wet, unnecessarily.

"Heather, should we use the SMART Decision Pad here?"

"I guess so, Mom. My goal is to get across the creek, right?"

"Right, but do you want to get across dry or wet?"

"Mom, that's silly—dry! Oh, I get it; I could check out the creek and maybe find a dry place ... like right over there!"

"Good girl!"

A year ago you would have shouted, "Heather, you're going to be soaked if you cross there. Come over here where there are rocks to walk on and we'll stay dry." Heather would have felt silly, and you would have felt good for giving her advice. Today, you helped Heather to pick a better path, and she became a tiny bit more resourceful because she—not you—came up with the solution. You taught her *how* to think, not *what* to think. You gave her a little more resourcefulness, and a little less PHD.

CHAPTER 3

LISTEN TO YOUR CHILD

'I've got to do something I like, or ... or ...'

The dark boy put the question to him he had not been able to ask himself.

'Or what?'

Johnny lifted his thin, fair face. His lips parted before he spoke.

'I just don't know. I can't think.'

Apparently the printer's boy did not know either. All he said was, 'More cheese?'

Then Johnny began to talk. He told all about the Laphams and how he somehow couldn't seem even to thank Cilla for the food she usually got to him. How cross and irritable he had become. How rude to people who told him they were sorry for him. He told about the burn, but with none of the belligerent arrogance with which he had been answering the questions kind people had put to him. As he talked to Rab, for the first time since the accident, he felt able to stand aside from his problems—see himself.

—Esther Forbes, Johnny Tremain

All Johnny did was listen—really listen—to Rab, and Rab poured his heart out. As psychologists we know all of the advice, techniques, and activities in this book will work best when you listen to your child. We've always believed that one of the most effective ways that parents can help their children succeed is conversing with them; it increases their language skills, reasoning abilities, and self-confidence. You can't coach your children to be can-do kids unless you show them—consistently and clearly—that you are listening to them. Smart Parenting *requires* good listening. In this chapter, we will show you how to actively listen to your child.

> Smart Parenting *requires* good listening.

As a child I (Kate) usually felt heard. I remember my parents listened to us and they also talked about the importance of listening. After family parties, they'd always ask us who had listened really well and get us to tell them why we thought so. It made us conscious of how much people like being with great listeners. Many of the adolescents I see professionally tell me that I'm the first adult who's ever truly listened to them. We think many children don't feel heard.

So make a point of really listening to your children. Start by setting the stage—it's hard to have a good conversation when you're being interrupted or when the television or even loud music is on. Many parents tell us that their best conversations with their children take place in the car. This can be a relaxed setting and a relaxed situation.

In our family, my mother drove me home from school everyday and, when I was around 13, this was talking time. We even had a little ritual: stop for a snack (a Diet Pepsi™ and a KitKat™ for me, coffee for my mother), then talk. I liked talking in the car because I felt relaxed. I didn't have to look at her—I could if I wanted to, but if I was talking about something kind of embarrassing (and lots of things are embarrassing when you're 13!), I could just stare straight ahead at the road. I didn't feel grilled—she'd just ask questions like "What is your teacher like?" and if I just said, "She's nice." or something, she'd say, "OK, but just remember I'm here if you want to talk." When I *did* talk, she really listened. I knew she was listening because of the look on her face and the way she said,

"Yes" and "Mm-hmm" and asked an occasional question, and how she moved her hands. She moved her hands so much (even as she was driving!) as she listened that I teased her about it. I enjoyed those talks in the car.

And I remember some of the *worst* conversations in our family taking place when my father was rushing off someplace and wanted to find out about my day before he left. That could feel like a police interrogation. He could be very abrupt: "What did you learn today?" When he was stressed, it showed in his tone of voice—he might as well have been saying, "Come on, come on, give me the data!" Now his advice to other busy, high-achieving parents is to relax! As a busy father, it took him awhile to learn to do this when he was with us kids, but it was worth the effort.

> We both advise postponing important conversations until you can concentrate and pay attention to your child in a relaxed way.

We both advise postponing important conversations until you can concentrate and pay attention to your child in a relaxed way. Children are very sensitive to stress; many are much better at picking up on it than the adults around them realize. Recently the CEO of a major corporation allowed his family to rate him as a parent, using the same sort of review process he gave himself at work, and then he let them share the results with reporters on National Public Radio's "Marketplace." One child said she didn't like talking to her father when he was stressed. "When my Dad is stressed, he spreads it around the family—it's like an infectious disease: The whole family gets stressed."

We've seen it happen. The harried parent wants to concentrate on essentials, which too often means just telling children what to do, rather than listening to the problem and helping them come up with a solution. This sends the message that you think your children can't come up with the solution themselves. Think of how you feel when you're upset and instead of listening someone just tells you what to do. Being heard and understood is as helpful and comforting to kids—and for many it's a rare experience.

Listen in day-to-day conversations, not just during serious talks about important matters. Instead of giving your own opinions, encourage children to give theirs. (Meals are a great time to do this.) If kids are accustomed to appeasing adults, you may have to coax them a bit and wait to get an answer. When we tested our ideas in schools, some children were initially quite intent on *avoiding* expressing their opinions. We especially remember one clever child who, when we kept asking, smiled innocently and said, "But what do *you* think? I'm just curious."

When an adult asks a question and is really interested in hearing the answer, some kids light up and can't talk fast enough. Others speak hesitantly, guardedly, or get tongue-tied. Sometimes when children are silent, they're thinking or trying to figure out how to say something. What follows a lengthy pause is often quite heartfelt. Children aren't as articulate as adults, and it can take them awhile to find the right words. If you patiently wait and listen with genuine interest, they just might find the words.

One of the most powerful ways to get kids talking and to really understand what they're saying is to use *active listening*, which is playing back what your child has just said, with empathy, not commentary or judgment. You rephrase what your child has said and let your tone of voice and your eyes reflect your child's feeling. For example, if your 12-year-old says, "I don't think I'll go out for football this season—a lot of the kids have grown much more than I have," you might ask, "You don't want to go out for the football team because the other kids are bigger than you are?" You've shown your child that you heard what he said—not just that other kids have grown but he feels relatively *smaller* than the others. That's active listening. Your child will appreciate it and maybe open up some more.

> "Yeah, but it's not that I'm worried about getting hurt. I just don't want to get cut from the team. What would my friends say?"

> "Sounds like you're worried about your friends rejecting you; that was probably my biggest fear when I was your age."

> "It was? Cool. I mean, you know what I'm feeling."

> **Most adults say they talk more and listen less to children than they should.**

Active listening helped you understand what your son really was afraid of—peer rejection. And your son felt your empathy. More importantly, active listening helped you bond with your child, who no longer feels alone with his concerns. Most adults say they talk more and listen less to children than they should. So if you are like most busy parents, you may need to make a conscious, extra effort to listen more.

See Chapter 13, Learn Active Listening, for several advanced listening activities that will help you learn the skills and teach your children.

CHAPTER 4

HAVE MEALS TOGETHER

"The single strongest predictor of academic achievement scores and low rates of behavior problems was amount of home-based family meal time. Meal time was a more powerful predictor than time spent in school, studying, and church, or participation in sports. This result held even when controlled for race, gender, education, age of parents, income and family size. American teenagers who had five or more dinners per week with a parent had higher rates of academic success, better psychological adjustment, lower rates of alcohol and drug use, and lower suicidal risk. Eating together surely is a good thing."

—Marshall P. Duke, Robyn Fivush,
Amber Lazarus, and Jennifer Bohanek,
Of Ketchup and Kin: Dinnertime Conversation
as a Major Source of Family Knowledge,
Family Adjustment, and Family Resilience[1]

THERE ARE PROBABLY MANY REASONS for the correlation between eating meals together and having happy, healthy children who achieve academically. Sharing ideas and experiences around the dinner table bonds families and brings people closer together—and it's stimulating to children. What analyzing ideas together as a family ultimately does for kids is help them to think on their own.

In her practice, Kate has seen the value of such family time—and the downside of parents who don't encourage conversation during meals. "So many times kids are told what they have to know, what they have to study. Children need to be encouraged to think on their own—and the dinner table is a perfect place for parents to do that." Meals together nourish more than the body. At meals, children learn language skills and practice social skills. Talking with each other and their parents at meals teaches children the art of conversation and lets them practice its give-and-take. Many people learn to be interesting talkers and good listeners at the family dinner table. In this chapter, we discuss ways to:

- Schedule meals and make time for them. (If you don't do this, it won't happen!)
- Plan the meals.
- Encourage everyone to talk.
- Instill good manners.

All children benefit from having meals as a family, but different children have different issues: some need to be encouraged to talk and some not to monopolize the conversation. And different families have different conversational styles and needs as well. So in this chapter, we'll offer examples from many variations of families.

> The point is simply for the family to talk in a pleasant, relaxed, but stimulating way.

What the conversations have in common is that they're relaxed and fun. We can't emphasize enough that the point is simply for the family to talk in a pleasant, relaxed, but stimulating way, *not* to have the gourmet meal of the century or the perfect Martha Stewart table settings—unless someone in the family sometime enjoys providing that sort of thing and has the time to do it! But if your family enjoys conversing most at McDonald's or by ordering takeout, by all means do that.

Schedule Meals Together

For many families, simply finding a time when everyone can get together is a challenge. So on Sunday or Monday, find out about schedules and other activities for the week and figure out times that will work. We encourage five nights a week, but if that's too much, start with one or two and increase it gradually. Make it fun and the children will want to do it more often.

Sunday dinner is a time many families enjoy spending together. There are apt to be fewer conflicting events on a Sunday—and people have all weekend to get other obligations out of the way. One family we know almost always has dinner together on Sunday night. So the children won't stress about homework during the meal or use it as an excuse to leave the table early, this family has a simple rule: get your homework done before Sunday dinner. Schedule meals together in a light-hearted way—if the schedule is too rigid, it will ruin the fun. Involve the children in the scheduling; they may think of ideas that would never occur to you. Some years ago, we read about a large family (with all the children in different after-school activities) that made *breakfast* their regular family meal. When the reporter asked how they had started the custom, they said that they were trying to figure out when they could have dinner together and one child said, "The only time no one has anything else going on is at 6:30 in the morning!" Another (who was always up then anyway) said, "Well, why don't we do it then?"

If that won't work for you, don't worry; you're the parent, *you* get the final say. After all, you're responsible for making it happen and some privileges come with that responsibility. But try to get your kids to suggest which will be family meals. That's what the Smart family did, agreeing on about 10 meals together weekly—breakfast early and dinner sometimes as late as 8 p.m. If any of us were hungry before dinnertime, we'd get a snack, but we'd try to eat when everyone was home.

One family we know always goes out for Saturday lunch together. It makes a fun break between errands and everyone always looks forward to it. Some families make a point of having a leisurely breakfast together once a week. I (Kate) remember that every Sunday when I was young our dad would make breakfast. He always made pancakes and shaped them into our initials and we felt so special and looked forward to it all week. And our dad enjoyed it, too. It gave our mom a break (part of the routine was that he and we kids always cleaned up, so she only had to tidy the kitchen), and he liked the ritual of having a regular time to just hang out and have fun with us kids.

Plan Meals

If you're not used to having many meals together as a family, we suggest that the parents put some thought into planning some, especially at first. After a while, when pleasant meals have become routine, you won't need to think about it so much, but at the beginning a little thought from you will make meals more fun for everyone. Involve your children in the planning; you might suggest that everyone come to the table with one fun topic to discuss. The topic can be absolutely anything: a question, a story, a fact, an event, an item from the news or a book or a movie—anything the *child* thinks would be interesting for everyone to talk about.

Be sure to plan the seating. You would plan the seating for a dinner party, so why not for your family? One friend of ours, always in demand as a guest at adult dinner parties because of her conversational skills (she's a good listener as well!), grew up in a rather formal Southern family. Her father was a diplomat, her parents entertained a lot, and their dining room table was huge. So when they had dinner as a family, they deliberately did not have regular seats, figuring if everyone sits in the same places (e.g., mother closest to the kitchen at one end of the dining room table, father at the other end, kids in the middle), then the conversations tend to be less interesting than if the seating is different every meal. The Smarts sat (and still do) at a round table for the same reason. When the family sits in a circle, it's easier for each member to make eye contact with the others and to talk.

Kids look forward to meals when something special happens. Some children find it fun to make decorations, like little place cards or placemats. I (Kate) remember that sometimes our mother would decorate the table with flowers or use the prettiest china and a tablecloth. Sometimes we did odd things, like all sit in the hammock and eat from plates in our laps. When Geoff and I were in high school, we sometimes made the dinner. For special occasions, we'd write out a menu on the computer, with different fancy fonts and then print out four copies.

CAFÉ SMART

Dinner menu

Appetizer
Puffed pastry filled with cheese and herbs

Salad
Tomato, mozzarella, basil, vinaigrette dressing

Entrée
Grilled chicken, green beans with almonds on top,
mashed potatoes

Dessert
Apple pie with cheddar cheese slices on the side,
vanilla ice cream

Some families like to dress up once per week, finding the effort makes conversation and manners a little nicer. Clean hands and faces and brushed hair are a must, whether the meal is formal or casual.

Whether you eat in or go out, give yourself the goal of staying at the table together, eating and talking, for at least one hour at dinner. Children don't open up in short units of time; they need a sense of relaxation and ease, and it may take them a while to adjust to the new dinner routine.

We suggest minimizing distractions. There should be no television on; it's hard to concentrate on the conversation with a TV on, even if it's in the background. Music is OK, if the volume is low and if it's something

It's family time, so no interruptions.

everyone likes or can at least tolerate. Many families, including ours, don't answer the phone, much less make calls, during dinner. We find that it disrupts the conversation too much. With so many distractions all day, many families tell us they insist on this rule at dinnertime: it's family time, so no interruptions. Everyone, including the kids, may be surprised at how relaxing it is *not* to multitask!

As for what to eat, plan something you think everyone (parents and kids) will like, without going to absurd lengths or extremes. For example, one extreme can be summed up by a parent who said, "My son won't eat vegetables." She always prepared one meal for herself and her husband, one for her quasi-vegetarian daughter, and one for her son. Another extreme is making everyone at the table eat everything on their plates: "You're not leaving this table until you finish those beets." Many adults can remember their parents making them stay at the table to finish cold, congealing, increasingly unappetizing food. One adult friend remembers being repulsed by the bean sprouts in the chop suey. They looked like worms to him. When his parents said he'd stay at the table until he ate them, he sat there for three hours—until his mother quietly threw them away and sent him to bed.

We suggest serving healthy, tasty meals, and encouraging, but not forcing children to stretch a little: "Try the fish and if you don't like it yet, maybe you'll like it when you're older."

Encourage Everyone to Talk

Conversation should involve everyone and be relaxed, pleasant, and fun. Your role as a parent is to monitor and guide it enough so that everyone gets to speak, but not so much that questions and discussions are like being called on or reprimanded in school. Many children need to be encouraged to talk. One of the best ways to do that is with good questions and attentive listening. Many adults don't know how to question children: "How was your day?" can work for older kids, but may be too broad for younger ones.

One mother we know explained, "Some topics are guaranteed to *end* conversations. A question like 'What did you do in school today?'

can be very confusing for young children because they have so many experiences in the course of a day that to be asked to give a simple answer to a huge question like that is overwhelming. That's why the answer to this question is so often 'Nothing.' Many adults don't realize how much there is going on from a young child's point of view in the course of a day."

So many important, fascinating things—all experienced intensely—happen in the course of a young child's day that broad, general questions are almost impossible to answer. So ask specific, interesting questions, maybe about a particular person or activity. To do that you'll need to know something about your child's day. If your child isn't talkative, do a little research. The best source, of course, is your child, but most schools supply schedules, newsletters, and other information that you can use to formulate interesting, informed questions.

Your children will probably say more if you make the questions open-ended, not to be answered by "Yes" or "No." For example, "It's a shame your teacher is out. What is the substitute like?" works better than "Is the substitute nice?" and "What do you think about the new dress code?" works better than "Are kids obeying the new dress code?" Many parents find that the best way to get a conversation going is to ask their kids their opinions about things. Questions asking for opinions are good because they can lead to in-depth discussions.

> **Your children will probably say more if you make the questions open-ended.**

If you want mealtime conversation to be relaxed and pleasant, we would also suggest *not* using the dinner table as the forum for questions like "Have you done your homework?" or "Do you have a test tomorrow?" As one mother put it, "Questions like that are *not* conversations." Deal with them before or after the meal. Most children do not like to be grilled!

The best way to keep a conversation going is to be attentive, so don't jump in and give your opinions while your child is talking, don't interrupt with your own feelings, and don't try to talk your child out of feelings. This is one way to show that you're interested and listening.

(Practice the lessons in Chapter 3.) When it's your turn to talk, by all means bring up topics that interest you and share your thoughts; kids want to know what their parents think and feel. Hypothetical questions can also be good conversation starters. "What would you do about X (*some* situation in your community) if you were the mayor?" "What would be your ideal way to spend a day?" "If you could go anywhere in the world, where would it be?"

Few things are more bonding or make a meal more fun than laughter. It's hard to give examples because what is one family's beloved, often-repeated joke is rarely funny to an outsider. That's part of the moment's appeal: only the people who were there remember and understand it, and it can often evoke such strong memories that later only a key word or phrase is needed to set the whole family laughing or at least smiling. "Steak sauce" is one of those phrases in the Smart family. Once we were all talking about some very serious, intellectual topic—the issues around bilingual education or something like that—and I (Kate) hadn't put the cap back on the steak sauce tightly enough. My brother picked up the bottle, shook it, and sauce sprayed all over: it hit the window, the wooden blinds, our faces and hair. We all burst out laughing. For years after that, when someone was about to open a bottle of something, someone else would say, "Steak sauce!" and we'd all crack up.

Allow Equal Attention and Time

To make mealtime conversation work, parents need to pay attention to everyone and give everyone equal time. Some children talk more than others and the quieter ones can feel left out or, worse, resentful. And yet those same kids can feel put on the spot if the conversation is directed at them. Nevertheless, we suggest parents encourage quieter kids to talk more. More verbal children need to learn to give others a chance to talk too. You can wait until the talker pauses and then, *if* you think someone else would like to talk, say something like "Suzy, what do you think about ____ (whatever the topic is)?" Or, if one child is dominating and another being left out, you can interrupt and say something like "Excuse me, John, how about wrapping up your point so we can hear from someone else?" Pay attention to body language:

when another child is fidgeting, moving his hands, or looking imploringly at the parents, it's probably time to intercede.

Sharing the floor is not just fair to everyone, the discussion will be more lively if it's an exchange rather than if one person conducts a monolog for 15 minutes. A real conversation as opposed to a speech, at its best, is a *dialog* among people: everyone talks, everyone listens, and most important, *all* the children can learn when they participate.

I (Kate) remember my dad and my brother becoming quite passionate as they discussed one of their favorite topics, politics. Often they would just talk over me because their voices were so loud. Sometimes I'd catch my Mom's eye and she'd say, "I think Kate has something to say." At times, I raised my hand as if I was in school! My father would apologize when that happened. Eventually everyone recognized the dynamic and I got to talk more. We even had a discussion about how to interject gracefully.

We're not suggesting that all conversation at meals be centered on the children. The adults need to talk to each other, too. It's also good for the children to see adults talking to each other, being interested in each other, sharing their thoughts and feelings, even if it's arguing. A lot of modeling goes on at meals: when children observe how their parents work things out, they learn.

Sometimes things got a little heated between the Smart parents at meals. When that happened, my brother and I would just eat really quietly and try to use our best manners and watch how they worked it out, how they compromised. Once my dad asked my mom if she had done something and she hadn't.

He said, "How come? Mary, this is important, we need this information."

"I'm sorry," she said. "I had to call the bank, and then I was on hold for a long time. Then I had a lot else to do and I figured I'd get to it tomorrow."

"This was top priority," he said, raising his voice. It was scary to hear my father raising his voice—and it was sad to see my mom upset.

"You know what?" she said. "I'll just have to do it tomorrow!" There were tears in her eyes. Then my dad felt bad.

He asked, "Are you feeling a little overwhelmed right now?"

She nodded. Then he said, in a nice voice, "How about if I take this? You're doing a lot and have so much on your plate right now. I can handle the call."

And then it was OK: we knew that even before they gave each other a hug.

We believe that it's fine for parents to argue or even fight in front of their kids, as long as they resolve differences appropriately in front of them, too. And it's OK if the kids argue at the table, too, as long as they learn to work through differences construc-

Don't leave the table angry.

tively. Don't leave the table angry. Children learn from listening and watching their parents talk to each other, and resolve problems.

Ask your children to come up with topics to discuss. For example, once Kate was doing a report on Renaissance meals. People ate pies with whole blackbirds in them, with sugared almond pastry on top, and she thought that was really disgusting. Telling about this led to a general conversation about what people had eaten on trips, which in turn led to different customs in different countries.

From fourth grade on, Kate and her brother Geoff were asked to bring an article to the table. The article had to be from *The Wall Street Journal, The New York Times,* or National Public Radio. Geoff now says:

> Mealtime, especially dinnertime, was one way I learned how to think on my feet. We talked about a lot of issues, but it was not the issue that mattered. What mattered was the dinnertime forum in which you had to be informed, formulate an argument articulately, and then have it tested.

> We were really encouraged to think by our parents. At mealtime, being asked, "What do you think?" constantly made me think more critically about the world. At school, you are asked to memorize and regurgitate. At home, we had a chance to formulate our own thoughts.

Kate learned a lot from these discussions, but in her early teens had more fun talking about people, relationships, biology, animals, and places. One father noted:

> Conversation starts easily when you (or ideally, the kids) throw out a topic—any topic—and you just let the kids say what they think. Almost any situation can lend itself to this approach. For example, the other night we were discussing a parent who started shouting at the coach during a soccer game. At dinner I asked the children what they thought when they saw this and that led to a discussion on proper adult behavior. Our kids are eager to say what they think and are delighted that someone actually cares to hear their ideas! This activity has opened windows to their thoughts for us—and given them the fundamental building blocks for articulating their ideas. It shows them that their thoughts count and that they can discuss anything that comes to mind.

We also believe that meals are wonderful times to teach moral values and help your children formulate their own. Pose questions with a moral component and have your children use the SMART Decision Pad to decide what to do.

> Meals are wonderful times to teach moral values.

I (Brad) once raised a dilemma I was having with a client at dinner. The client, a CEO, had asked me to do something highly unethical (change my assessment conclusion about someone so the CEO could fire him). I asked Kate and Geoff what they thought I should do. This situation was: the CEO requested something I wouldn't do. The kids both started talking about what I could say to the CEO to get him to withdraw his unethical request. But good decision making means having a clear goal before thinking of solutions, so I asked them to clarify the goal. Eventually they agreed that the goal was for me to retain my client relationship without doing anything unethical. Then they started thinking of options—what I could say to change the CEO's mind. But all the options seemed like a waste of time. Even if the CEO decided I didn't have to change my report, I'd be left with doubts about the CEO's ethics. Then the kids said, "Your goal should be to only work with honest, ethical clients! Why would you want to keep this client?" I had already decided to end the relationship, but the dinner conversation showed Kate and Geoff the importance of clarifying the goal before thinking of ways to achieve it—and it drove home the importance of ethics.

Require Good Manners

We'll never forget one family that came to our house. As the children ran around the room and one jumped up and down on the small antique sofa in the corner, the mother said mildly, "My children have no manners at all." We remember being really puzzled about where she thought good manners came from. Did she think manners were genetic?

We believe that as soon as children can talk, they're old enough to start learning about table manners. When it would probably be OK to interrupt and when it would not, for example, takes years to learn—it's not something anyone knows instinctively. Meals are a good place to gradually teach children this skill. We've seen parents do it by saying things like "Hold on just one second. Let me just finish my conversation with Aunt Peg and then we'll talk about Barney." Or, in a very nice tone, as though explaining something, "Oh, I can see you're feeling frustrated right now because you really want to say something, but it's rude to interrupt so I'm going to finish my conversation and then we'll talk about what you want to talk about."

Teaching children can have a good effect on parents, too. Adults who get overexcited in conversation and tend to interrupt will do it less when they know they are trying to model good manners for their children—and the conversation will be more pleasant for everyone.

Not interrupting and good basic table manners (such as not eating with your hands, not throwing food, not chewing with your mouth open, and using a napkin frequently) also make for a much more pleasant meal. We've noticed that people are nicer to each other when they are using good table manners. When people hold and move their bodies formally and politely, they tend to speak formally and politely and consider other people and their feelings more too.

> People are nicer to each other when they are using good table manners.

Scheduling meals together may seem impossible! But hundreds of parents have mustered their resourcefulness and found meals together worth the effort.

Note

1. Marshall P. Duke, Robyn Fivush, Amber Lazarus, and Jennifer Bohanek, *Of Ketchup and Kin: Dinnertime Conversations as a Major Source of Family Knowledge, Family Adjustment, and Family Resilience*. Atlanta: Emory University, Center for Myth and Ritual in American Life, Working Paper 26, May 2003.

PART TWO

Smart Parenting Activities for Kids

CHAPTER 5

LEARN SOMETHING TOGETHER

Jim Lochner first became interested in astronomy in the second grade when he came across The Golden Book of Astronomy. *His father explained the picture of Newton's Third Law and on subsequent nights he and his father went out with a 1.4-inch refractor telescope. Looking upon the rings of Saturn and the Orion Nebula convinced Jim he had found a career. [He is now a NASA astrophysicist at the Guest Observer Facility for the Rossi X-ray Timing Explorer (RXTE).]*

—Dr. Jim Lochner, Stories and Science, Biography[1]

LEARNING SOMETHING TOGETHER CAN be intellectually and emotionally stimulating for your child and you—as well as just plain fun. The two of you will be peers in the sense that you are equally new to the skill or topic, and the parent will become both a cheerleader and coach who makes learning more exciting. You're not necessarily the teacher, but a fellow student. Going through learning experiences together will deepen the connection between you and your child, giving him or her confidence to try things, and provide numerous opportunities for you to coach your child to be more resourceful.

This chapter gives examples and tips for ways to learn with your child. These are the foundations for creating a positive learning experience:

- Let your child choose something that he or she wants to learn. The goal is to find something that will passionately interest him, something not too challenging, not too easy.

- Allow enough time.

- Adjust your learning style to match your child's.

- Check your child's interest level frequently.

- Model good learning skills. As you learn, you will be your child's cheerleader, but you'll also be a role model for asking questions, being attentive, demonstrating resourcefulness, and displaying other important learning skills.

- Stick with whatever you're learning yourself and encourage your child to stick with it, too.

Learn Something Together

Time: From 30 minutes to several hours. This could be something you do once or an ongoing activity, something you do together once a week until you've mastered the skill or something for which you develop a lifelong love.

Venue: Anywhere—at home, on a boat, at a riding stable.... It depends completely upon what you and your child have decided you want to learn together.

Let Your Child Choose What to Learn

What you learn together can be as simple or as elaborate as you and your child want it to be. You can learn to speak a new language, swim, ride a horse, fly a plane—anything that passionately interests your child. Your child's interest is more important than yours in this effort. We have one Boston friend who was always unsuccessfully urging her children to join the Metropolitan Boating Club, which offered free sailing lessons. She told us, "I thought it would be so nice for Miranda and Charles if they learned to sail so we could enjoy sailing as a family. Now I realize that *I* was the one it would have been nice for. The kids hated sailing!"

Our main advice, what we want to emphasize: let your kids pick the learning activities. For instance, I (Brad) was never particularly interested in horses, but Kate was, so we learned to ride together. Even if it's something you don't really enjoy, the bonding makes it worth it. And if your child is more interested than you, she is apt to be more resourceful than you. For example, I was not very interested in learning different breeds of horses but Kate was, so she figured out we could learn by visiting farms, talking with breeders, reading books, and going to horse shows.

How do you find out what your child would like to do? Some children will tell you if you ask them. Others may reveal a talent or interest by accident, during another activity: be alert for things as they come up—and when something does, make a mental note or even write it down. Once when I was pitching a baseball to Geoff, Kate's older brother, so he could practice batting, Kate asked, "Can I take a swing at it?" She got a solid hit on her first try. I asked if she'd like to start going to the batting cages with Geoff and me on Saturdays. She said she would and next season she was the only girl on the town's Little League team.

Conversations with your child can also suggest things you might learn together. If, for example, your child has talked about being afraid on the bus, you could ask if she'd like to take a self-defense class with you. If you've never made a martial arts move in your life, that can be a plus, because you'll be learning something together.

One of our father-son activities was learning to fly gliders. (A glider is a plane without an engine; it is usually towed into the air by an airplane, and then the glider pilot releases the tow rope.) Geoff said, "By learning something together as equals, I found myself thinking a lot more for myself than I would have if my father had been an ace." Geoff initiated this activity when he saw an ad for a free glider ride at a local airport. The activity sounded a little risky, but we soon learned the gliding community's mantra, "The most dangerous part of gliding is the drive to and from the airport." We were concerned about safety, figured out ways to judge it and improve it, and soon concluded that it *can be* a dangerous sport and would require us to be very resourceful to participate safely. Geoff and I were peers, together clarifying goals ("Pop, trying to fly out 15 miles and back is too dangerous today, given wind conditions, so let's stay within a five-mile radius") and options ("In case we get strong updrafts that might take us to 15,000 feet, we should have a back-up supply of oxygen").

SMART Decision Pad
Goal: Land Safely

OPTION 1: LAND ON THE RUNWAY	
<u>Advantages</u>	<u>Disadvantages</u>
Long solid surface with no obstacles.	In the fog we could miss it and crash in the quarry.
OPTION 2: LAND ON THE SKI HILL	
Good visibility.	Might hit skiers.
Could pick a landing area with no trees.	
OPTION 3: LAND IN AN OPEN FIELD	
Good visibility.	Could hit a concealed boulder
It's flat.	or fence and get hurt.
No people or animals are in it.	

Figure 5-1. Decision pad for landing glider

Once, when fog concealed the runway west of the Grand Teton Mountains, we had half an hour to consider our options for landing. We considered landing on the fog-bound runway only a few yards from a deep quarry, on a road, on the slippery ski hill, or in an open field. The SMART Decision Pad wasn't theoretical—it was an intensely practical roadmap that saved our skins. We agreed to land in an open snowy field. Even though a boulder just beneath the surface of the snow could bang us up, it was the best—or least bad—option. But when the wind blew the fog enough to give us a glimpse of one end of the runway, we quickly reassessed our options and decided to land there, betting that the owners of the gliding operation would have turned on the runway lights. (They had, fortunately.)

Sometimes you can get your child on the road to learning something new by just following his or her lead and letting things evolve naturally. When an American colleague was a child during the Cold War, a Russian was always the world chess champion—until a young American named Bobby Fischer beat Boris Spassky. Our colleague recalls:

I was around nine, and there was an East vs. West playoff and a young American kid won! I got interested in the game: I remember thinking, "The next champ could be me!"

My friend Emil and I started playing together. We knew how to move the pieces, but didn't understand the game at a strategic level. We started playing with each other regularly, but neither one of us was very good. Then we started playing Emil's father. We would take turns playing with him, watch the other person play, try to catch their bad moves, understand their good moves. Emil's father didn't really say that much—he just played. Sometimes when we made a bad move, he might say, "Are you sure you want to do that?"

But other than that, he left it up to us to figure out. What he did was donate his time and attention. He played with us, and we got better by playing more.

We also started doing the chess puzzles in the newspaper: "chess puzzle in three moves—checkmate in three moves." We'd set up the board (Emil would be black and I'd be white) and we'd try to figure out what the check-

mate was. The interesting thing is that Emil and I were, and even to this day are, very even in our skills, but his dad is not that good. That's why we were able to play his dad and, as we got better, beat him..

Chess affects everything I do, in terms of how I think and plan. It taught me not to do the first thing that comes to mind, but to look at all the different options and anticipate all the implications.

—Stephen Brobst, Chief Technology Officer, Teradata, a division of NCR Corporation

No one suggested that Stephen play chess as a learning activity; it just happened. If an interest of your child's evolves into a passion, encourage it! If you're going to learn something together, make it a moderate challenge. If it's too easy, your child will lose interest; if it's too hard, it can be frustrating and so discouraging that your child may want to give up. If you're not sure about challenging your child, it's probably better to start with something on the easy end of the spectrum, so the activity will build confidence. You can always add challenges.

> If you're going to learn something together, make it a moderate challenge.

If you discover along the way that something is way too hard, just stop and choose something else. It's better to stop before your child gets so frustrated that he or she wants to give up. Later in the chapter, we'll give some examples of when to give up and when to urge your child to keep going.

Allow Enough Time

Let your child learn at his or her own pace. In school, many children are forced to work either more slowly or more quickly than they would like to. So, for most children, the chance to learn something at the pace that's most comfortable for them—not for the teacher or some other adult—is a welcome

Let your child set the pace.

break from being rushed along or waiting for slower learners. Even if you're having a hard time catching on or you find yourself getting impatient, let your child set the pace.

If you have a time limitation, we suggest that you announce it beforehand and remind your child if you've got something on your schedule. Then announce when the time is halfway over and also at the three-quarters mark.

Setting the parameters at the beginning will help both when your child is having so much fun that she doesn't want to stop or when she's trying to complete something that's more challenging. Before you begin, say something like "I need to get back to work at four, so we'll do this for an hour" or "The lesson will probably last for about 45 minutes." This is good for many reasons: children have a harder time with transitions than most adults, so it's a good idea to prepare them for stopping, especially if they're having a really good time.

The 15-minute reminder allows your child to go into preparing-to-stop mode; even if he can't tell time, he probably knows that 15 minutes means almost but not quite time to stop. Children react better to this notice than to a sudden announcement that the time is up. Most of us have had the experience of being at an amusement park or a swimming pool and hearing parents say abruptly, "OK, kids, get your stuff, we're leaving *now!*"

Often, the response to an announcement like that is screaming or the long drawn-out "No-oo-oo!" If the parents had prepared for the departure gradually ("We're leaving in 15 minutes, so if you want to have one more ride, you should probably get in line now."), the children would be more likely to leave gracefully, because they'd feel more prepared and more in control.

Adjust Your Learning Style to Match Your Child's

Once you have chosen an activity, adjust your learning style to match your child's. The Smarts, for example, all learn quite differently. Kate is quite visual, preferring to watch someone do something and then do it herself. Geoff is typically logical, preferring step-by-step instructions. Brad is usually experimental, preferring to "just push the buttons and see if it works." Mary likes a lot of dialog. When I (Brad) learn with Kate or Geoff, I restrain myself and try to learn the way they learn. We urge you to do the same with your children. For example, if your natural tendency would be to ignore an instruction manual while hooking up a piece of equipment, and you have a logical, step-by-step child, your child could read the instructions aloud while you follow them, discussing any questions about them.

Check Your Child's Interest Level Frequently

Some children can be hard to read—especially if they sense that an activity is important to a parent and want to please that parent. So, pay attention for signs of waning interest (such as wandering eyes or fidgeting); if you aren't sure if your child is getting tired, or bored, or unable to concentrate, ask. Some children will respond to blunt questions like "Do you want to stop now?" with an emphatic "Yes!" Sometimes an indirect approach will work better with another child: "It's one o'clock now—when/what time would you like to stop?," "How are you feeling about this now?," "What do you think?," or "How is this working for you?" All of these approaches can give your child a graceful out if she's getting bored or tired.

> If the child is really ready to stop, just stop.

If a child *is* losing interest, you can either encourage her to persevere or give her an out. Of course, your choice depends on your child and the situation. There are times when it's best to let a child stop. If you've arranged the activity as a special treat, a sensitive child may not want to hurt your feelings or disappoint you by saying she wants to go home. If your child is really ready to stop, just stop. If you do it the right way, your child is far more likely to go back to the activity later and succeed then, as opposed to giving up on the task permanently. Remember, too, that it can be better for your child to learn something in three or four sessions and stay interested, excited, and comfortable than for you to try to get through it in one session and bore or tire your child.

But the same advice doesn't apply if you are the one losing interest! If your child is really interested and excited by what the two of you are doing but *you* are not, keep doing it if you can.

Be a Good Learning Role Model

One of the best ways to foster learning is to model good learning behavior. For example, you can make learning more interesting by treating your child with a positive attitude and energy, praising each sign of progress he or she shows.

Tell your child that there is no such thing as a stupid question and back up this statement whenever you can. The best way to do this is to actively encourage questions, take them seriously when you answer them, and ask questions yourself. When someone is answering a question, listen attentively. Let your body language—looking at the speaker, nodding your head, responding verbally and nonverbally to the explanation—show your child how hard you are listening. If you are attentive to explanations, your child is likely to follow your lead and do the same. And this will be the case not just while the two of you are doing some activity, but whenever your child is in a new situation or learning a new skill.

You can model learning even if you haven't actually mastered the skill you two are learning. When Geoff, Kate, and I (Brad) were learning to water-ski, I fell down far more often than they did—and that was good for all of us. When you fall down or fail, you can show children that it's OK to fail, as long as you learn from your failures and you try again. And if your child learns how to do something faster or better than you (which often happens when the child has more

> When you fall down or fail, you can show children that it's OK to fail.

interest in the skill or topic than the parent) and can say, "Here, Mom, I think this is what he means" or "Dad, I think the instructions are referring to this part," your child's confidence will get a big boost.

Encourage Your Children's Learning by Praising Their Progress

Your sincere, undivided attention is powerful encouragement, so pay attention—pay lots of attention—and be obvious about it. Praise your children whenever they deserve it—with your words, your gestures, and your facial expressions. Be a cheerleader: when your child succeeds at a task or a step, say something and make it as specific as possible: "You made that turn really well!," "That was a smart move," "Your pronunciation is perfect," or "You figured out a terrific way to substitute materials and it worked!" When your child does something extra special, make a fuss—give her a high-five, jump up and down, hug her.

You can also use praise and encouragement to push your child a little if you suspect that her confidence or energy are flagging but you feel that she really *can* do it and will feel better about herself if she does. If that's the case, you can say something like this, in a pleasant, encouraging voice, "Keep going, you're doing great! Can you do just one more minute? One more time?"

Sometimes showing understanding and allowing the child to take a little break is the best form of encouragement. If, for example, you and your child are learning to swim and the child swallows a huge gulp of chlorine water and screams, "I want to get out!," you could say, "OK, let's take a break."

What you do after the break depends on your child and how scared she is. Some kids will want to get right back into the water. Others might need a little encouragement: "This time I'll be right here," "Let's try this again and this time I'll hold you," or "How about if you just play on the steps in the water?"

You can break a difficult task into smaller, more manageable bites. Our friend Mike remembers his mother doing this when he was afraid to climb to the top of a 100-foot tower. She suggested that he climb 10 steps, not all the way to the top: "Go as far as you feel comfortable," she told him. Then, when he stopped climbing, she said, "Good job! Oh, you went ten steps—how about one more?" A year later he finally made it to the top but, as he recalls, "With that sort of gentle pushing and encouragement by my mom, I pushed myself and remained in the safety zone. I didn't *feel* forced—we both agreed on how much farther I should go—but the encouragement was necessary. Without it I would have given up." Using encouragement and praise to push your child a little bit further is a lot more effective then forcing your child, getting angry, or being sarcastic.

How Not to Encourage Your Child

We would not be including a negative section if we had not heard or seen a thousand things parents said or did that deflated their children's initiative, sucking out their can-do spirit. Here are just a few examples:

- "Honestly, Johnny, sometimes I think you have no brains at all!"
- "Do it *now*!"
- "Don't wuss out."
- "Don't be a wimp."
- "This vacation is over right now if you don't try."
- "Don't be a chicken."
- "What's wrong with you?"
- "You get back in that water right now."
- "No allowance for you if you don't do this!"
- "You will do this and you will do it right and you will do it now."

Here are two more things to avoid:

- Don't make comparisons to siblings or friends. This will make your child angry at you and resentful of the sibling or friend (even though he or she hasn't done anything to deserve it).
- Don't make threats. You may think they're encouraging, but really they will just frighten your child and make him or her resentful.

Instead, encourage your child by using sincere praise and serving as a positive role model. That's how Stephen, the engineer who was a chess fanatic as a child, taught his nephew Ryan when he was only five years old:

> I don't believe in letting the other person win, so to make it even for Ryan, I took pieces off my side. At first I played without my queen, rooks, and bishops—I played with skill, but with a handicap. As Ryan got better, I gave up fewer pieces: now I only give up my queen. When Ryan won, I'd smile, shake his hand, and congratulate him.
>
> When he did well, I said things like "That was a good move; I didn't see that" or "Have you thought about what I'll do if you make that move?" Ryan knew that I genuinely wanted him to learn and enjoy the game.
>
> It was something to see him go from just knowing how to move the pieces to thinking strategically and understanding the concept of giving up something in the present to get something better later. That's a difficult yet important concept for a small kid. Ryan is now six, and when I visit the first thing he says is "Uncle Steve, do you want to play chess?"

Stick with It

Your child may choose an interest that takes months or years to master. If so, you'll undoubtedly encounter moments that are hard or boring or even frightening for one or both of you. Sticking with something (unless it's impossible or unsafe) through the hard patches is good for your child in several ways—building confidence, creating a can-do attitude, and proving that persistence pays off.

> It's up to you to help your child get over the rough spots, whether boredom, frustration, or fear.

It's important for the parent to stick with the activity as well; abandoning it sends the wrong message, teaching children that it's OK to quit. We urge you to stick with whatever it is you're learning, even if your child wants to quit prematurely. It's up to you to help your child get over the rough spots, whether boredom, frustration, or fear. This will help your child to learn how to deal with these feelings and obstacles in general.

For example, suppose it's a week after your child has swallowed a lot of water at the pool. You might say something like "It's time for your swim lesson. Last week you gave it a really good effort, I know it must have been scary when you gulped that water. What can we do today so that you feel safe?" (Notice that there is no choice about whether or not you're going back to the pool: that's just assumed.) He may say, "Can I try it with my swim fins on?" Or, you may suggest going into the water too: "This time I'll be standing right next to you every second." He will understand that he will be able to grab one of your arms and *not* swallow water, so he'll get back into having fun.

After you empathize ("I know it was scary!"), encourage your child to decide on a solution. That way, you build both confidence and resourcefulness. This conversation should take place in private, before you leave the house or begin the activity. If the trauma has been severe, going back may be a long process.

I (Kate) remember such an experience from my youth, playing baseball. I actually broke my jaw during one of the practices. The pitcher threw the ball at me, but I couldn't see it because the sun was glaring in my face. My mom threw up when she saw me. I remember looking in the mirror and just sobbing—my face looked distorted, my jaw was hanging down, I looked horrible, grotesque. I recovered, but was afraid to play again. My parents said I could do whatever I wanted, but my dad said, "Don't decide yet." I used the SMART Decision Pad a few times in the next month and finally donned a catcher's mask and asked my dad to *slowly* toss me balls. He started with a soft foam ball. Gradual steps and words of encouragement motivated me to stick with it.

> Gradual steps and words of encouragement motivated me to stick with it.

I finally felt comfortable hitting and fielding balls, but I said, "I'll look weird wearing a catcher's mask!" My dad didn't buy it. But instead of saying so, he asked me to write down the pluses and minuses of looking, as he put it, "different." I figured there would be some wisecracks, but I knew my teammates would be nice.

A couple of months later, there was a game with another team. As usual, I was the only girl on the field. When I came up to bat, the coach on the other team yelled to everyone in the outfield to come in. Everyone heard him shouting, "Come in, come in, it's the girl!" Nice. The pitch came right at me—right at my face—and I belted it over their heads.

That was the only home run I hit during my entire four years in Little League, but it was a huge confidence booster—and it would never have happened without all the practice and encouragement to stick with it I got from my parents. Had they forced me to "get back on the horse," I would have refused.

Note

1. National Aeronautics and Space Administration, Goddard Space Flight Center, imagine.gsfc.nasa.gov/docs/features/bios/lochner/lochner.html.

IMAGINE IT, PLAN IT, BUILD IT

Funny presents, some of them would have been defects to other eyes, were ornaments to grandma's—for the children's gifts were all their own. Every stitch Daisy's patient little fingers had put into the handkerchief she hemmed was better than embroidery to Mrs. March; Demi's shoe-box was a miracle of mechanical skill, though the cover wouldn't shut; Rob's footstool had a wiggle in its uneven legs, that she declared was very soothing ....

—*Louisa May Alcott,* Little Women[1]

MELIA EARHART ONCE RODE A roller coaster at a state fair and wanted to do it again, but there were no roller coasters in the small town where she was staying with her grandparents. So she convinced her uncle, her sister, and a boy who lived in the neighborhood to help her build one. Her idea was simple: construct a track that went from the top of a tool shed to the ground. As Amelia's sister Pidge later told a biographer, the children and their uncle hammered boards together for the track and greased it with lard. They used an empty wooden crate for the car. Because it had been her idea, they all agreed that Amelia could have the first ride.

The car careened down the track and tumbled at the bottom. Amelia jumped up, eyes shining, and said, "Oh, Pidge, it's just like flying!" Pidge didn't say who did what, just that the idea was Amelia's. Her uncle was good at letting the children direct things, while he was more of a helper. Little did he realize that helping Amelia develop her can-do spirit would result in her becoming one of the world's most famous aviators.

That's exactly how a child should remember your role in a building activity, whatever you actually end up doing or not doing. Your role as a helper in building involves doing the following:

- Use your child's idea.

- Make a plan. Let your child figure out how to turn his idea into something he can actually bring to life. You may need to guide him

Imagine It, Plan It, Build It

Time: 30 minutes to several hours, even a day, depending upon what you decide to build. This activity can be as simple or as elaborate as you care to make it.

Props/Equipment Required: What you will need depends upon what you build.

Venue: At home, either inside or outside. You may also need to go shopping to get materials.

with questions and occasional suggestions and to find or buy materials.

- Build it. Help with the actual building, *if* your child needs your help. If not, just be there as coach, appreciative audience, and safety inspector.

Use Your Child's Idea

The idea for the building activity should come from your child. Many children don't need help to think of ideas; they usually have ideas or can come up with some if their parents give them a chance. But if it's hard for your child to think of something he or she is excited about building, try brainstorming. Ask questions and listen with interest to all of the answers. As we discussed in an earlier chapter, during brainstorming even impractical ideas are acceptable. Asking questions can also be a good way for you to make an idea more practical or safer.

> If it's hard for your child to think of something, try brainstorming.

For example, before Amelia Earhart built the roller coaster, perhaps her goal was to build something that would enable her to "fly." An airplane would have been impractical and unsafe. So, her uncle could have asked what *else* she could build that would feel like flying and perhaps she would have thought about building a swing set, a bike with wings, or a stationary model of an airplane. She chose to build a roller coaster, a half-scale replica of which is displayed outside the Amelia Earhart Museum in Atchison, Kansas.

Sometimes it's easier for children to think of ideas if you ask questions about specific activities or places. One client asked his daughter if there was anything she'd like to play on that they didn't have in their yard and she thought of a swing. When Kate had to invent something for a school project, she couldn't think of anything, so I asked her to look around her room, "Is there anything here you could add onto or change? Is there anything you wish you had that would make your life easier?" "Maybe something to feed my fish," she replied. What we came up with was pretty useless, but we had fun thinking of it and it was easy to make—a board and two hinges. Strings attached to fish hooks kept the hinges suspended over the water (as shown in the illustration).

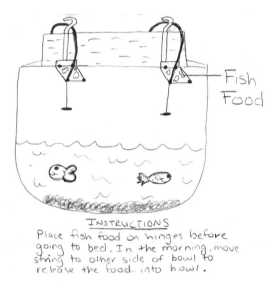

Fish Food

INSTRUCTIONS
Place fish food on hinges before going to bed. In the morning, move string to other side of bowl to release the food into bowl.

It didn't really save any *time*, Kate remembers, but it was fun to use the invention rather than to sprinkle the fish food on top of the water ... and it was entertaining to see how friends reacted to it, too. Whenever people first saw it, they'd ask, "What is that thing on top of your fish bowl? Is that so the fish don't jump out?" Most of all, it was satisfying for her to build something, creating a gadget herself.

Make a Plan

Figuring out how to turn an idea into a three-dimensional object is harder for some kids than thinking of an idea. A lot of time can be wasted unnecessarily, and that can discourage kids. Adults can really help in the planning, but need to be subtle and guide children to practical solutions with questions like "How else could you do that?" rather than opinions such as "I don't think that will work—why don't you try making it out of cardboard?" Offering too many opinions or suggestions implies that the child can't think of a solution without help and it can throw cold water on an enthusiastic child's vision.

Most children are excited at the idea of building something they really want and will enjoy planning it too, as long as they are making decisions and the planning phase doesn't go on for too long. We have seen children's initial enthusiasm—especially younger children's—far outstrip their patience. It's up to the adult to recommend ways to limit the activity, if the child's first ideas will take longer than his or her interest will last.

I (Brad) remember thinking that the "fun little Swiss family Robinson tree house" eight-year-old Kate described—complete with windows, wood-burning stove, and chimney— sounded so complicated that it would take a month to build and that she'd lose interest long before it was done. So, through questions, I suggested that we start by building a platform; we actually ended with a platform plus sides, but I let Kate discover for herself that for her, that was enough.

Another parent also used questions to realistically limit his seven-year-old daughter's project. Building something together was their first Smart Parenting activity. Jessica wanted a house for her tiny stuffed animals. Her father knew that buying, cutting, and hammering lumber would take too long for her, so he asked her what she could use to make the house. He was surprised by how many materials she thought of. "I didn't tell her what to do; I just kept asking questions. She thought of using shoeboxes and made all the other decisions on her own, too. We had a lot of fun doing this together, and I know she felt more inclined to figure things out on her own afterwards." Jessica's comment was shorter: "I like being the boss and Dad the helper. It's more fun than just being a helper."

> "I like being the boss and Dad the helper. It's more fun than just being a helper."

For some children, planning and getting started are both a lot easier when they have the materials in front of them. Our friend Meg Corcoran, an executive turned full-time mom, has two boys, ages 11 and 13. Her younger son, Scotty, was easily frustrated: "If he doesn't see a clear way to do something right away, he can't seem to do it at all," Meg said, and this worried her. When they tried this activity, she decided *not* to tell him what to do—or even make any suggestions—to see what would happen.

Scotty had a school project that required he build a model of a plant. He'd chosen the goldenrod and researched it without any trouble. Going online, he had found all of the information he needed, but seemed helpless when it came to actually making the model.

He was slouched over the kitchen table, his head in his hands, kind of shaking his head and saying, "It's too much. I can't do it."

"Show me some pictures," I said. I knew he had found lots on the Internet. That's all I said: then I just sat there and waited. He came back with a small stack of printouts. We looked at them together, and I said, "How could you make that?"

He didn't know, he couldn't think of anything.

"Well, what part of it would be the easiest to make?"

He pointed to the stalk, "That. It's tall and thin."

"What do we have (I don't want to spend a lot of money on this, Scotty) that you could use to make it?"

Once he started looking around the house at objects, he thought of lots of ideas, and when we looked in my craft box, he found pipe cleaners and started to get excited.

"They'd be perfect. I could twist some together for the main stalk and use single ones for the branches!" he said. Once he had thought of that, the rest of the plan was easy.

Build It

When your child has a plan and materials, he or she will probably only need you as an appreciative audience—or to do what one child later described as "the hard hammering." For example, when Meg's questions had helped Scotty see how he could make the stalks and he had picked out some green felt for the leaves, he couldn't wait to get started. He didn't need her help any more. They set things up on the kitchen table; he worked independently while Meg made dinner and answered the phone.

That was great because I could keep an eye on things, and be there for him if he needed me, without being as tempted to jump in. I love doing stuff like this, so sometimes it's hard for me not to just make whatever the kids are working on myself or make suggestions. But that day, I didn't. I forced myself to back off and, once he was working, not to make suggestions— even when I had a really good idea. I just praised what *he* had done.

Even when your child is working independently, we urge you to stay close enough to see if coaching is needed and to praise your child's progress. Praise and encouragement are crucial parts of this activity.

> Praise and encouragement are crucial parts of this activity.

We remember one couple who asked their children to choose a project; the kids decided to assemble chair-and-desk sets for their rooms. When the children started actually building the chairs, the parents went upstairs and left them to it, thinking they were encouraging resourcefulness by being hands-off. Luckily, they asked for feedback afterwards and were surprised when one of the children said, "It seemed like you just didn't have time to put them together yourselves, so you made us do it."

If you leave your children alone, you'll also miss one of the most interesting things about the activities: seeing what your children do when they're allowed to figure things out on their own. As Meg said:

> It was actually really interesting to see how Scotty created his goldenrod model. When he was gluing on the leaves, he did it completely differently than I would have. I would have put the whole leaf on the stalk, but he put just the leaves on so that they just kind of flopped down, in a very natural way. He spent almost six hours on that project—once he gets going, he goes! And it was beautiful when he was all done. I remember being so proud: that he had made it himself, that all the ideas were his—and it looked so beautiful! I think he was proud of it, too. It was the first project he ever made all by himself.

Of course, it's great when something comes out this well, but even if a project has flaws, it can still be fun to build and satisfying for your child to do it by herself with you as her coach. Parents rob their children of both satisfaction and initiative when they step in and *make* projects turn out perfect. Let your child do things her own way, even if that means letting her make mistakes. How else will she learn? Meg went on to say:

> I think it's really hard for parents *not* to tell their children what to do. For me it is, anyway; I've been telling them how to do things since they were born! But I'm learning to bite my tongue. It practically had holes in it by the end of the five-in-one foosball table my older son and I made from a kit after Scotty's goldenrod project. I do have my own ideas about how something should be done—and, although it's really interesting to see how different theirs are, and I want them to learn to think for themselves—guess what? It's still hard for me to admit that their ideas are as good as mine. It's hard, but it's worth it. After that one activity it was easier for Scotty to start projects on his own.

> **Parents rob their children of both satisfaction and initiative when they step in and *make* projects turn out perfect.**

Building something with a trusted grown-up is an experience many people remember fondly for the rest of their lives. If you think back to your own childhood, you may remember building something with a parent; but chances are, you were the helper and the parent was the one making most of the decisions. You'll be giving your child an experience that is just as warm, just as bonding, but maybe even more valuable, and definitely more fun, because your child will come up with most of the ideas. You'll be the helper. And you won't just be helping her build something; you'll be helping her become more resourceful.

If you and your child enjoy making things, "Imagine It, Plan It, Build It" could be one of your first Smart Parenting activities. Building something together is a great way to encourage kids to figure things out for themselves, because the questions that come up are so tangible and the results of the answers are so immediate and concrete.

Note

1. Louisa May Alcott, *Little Women*. Reissue edition. New York: Puffin Books, 1997.

CHAPTER 7

FIX SOMETHING TOGETHER

"The headmaster of my high school (Concord Academy) once met two young women—both, as it turned out, Smith graduates—standing helplessly by the side of the road. They were beside themselves because their car had a flat tire and they didn't know what to do. At that moment, he decided: 'No one is ever going to graduate from my school without knowing how to put on a spare tire.' So he had a class for seniors that taught us to fix things—that class made a big impression on me. It gave me the attitude that nothing is ever too hard, that if you take the time to analyze and understand a problem you really can do just about anything. This has stayed with me, and with many of my friends, too. We always took pride in the fact that we—unlike many women of our generation—could make household repairs and do anything else we set our minds to!"

—*Fiona, architect*

THIS IS THE CAN-DO ATTITUDE **you'll be giving** your children when you fix things together. Fixing things helps children feel competent, shows them that they can solve problems on their own, and makes them more resourceful. Of course, many of the other activities in this book have similar benefits—but there is an immediacy and a tangibility about fixing something that was broken that's *very satisfying* to kids. The relationship between cause and effect is so direct: you see the results right away.

Fixing things can also be reassuring. It shows children that there are ways to make almost *anything* better and that, in turn, gives them one more reason to have an optimistic, can-do zest for life. If you're not handy around the house, don't worry: you may be surprised by how resourceful you and your child are—and how quickly you can learn. Our definition of "broken" also includes things like hair with bubblegum in it.

This activity is often most satisfying, and most fun, when it happens spontaneously—when something gets broken and you and your child decide to fix it. In this chapter, we give examples and ideas for doing the following:

- Find something that will be satisfying for your child to fix—ideally, something your child cares about that has just broken.
- Research or figure out how to fix it. Your child will do this: you'll just be the helper who is asking questions.
- Fix it. You will probably do this together.

Fix Something Together

Time: 15 minutes to an hour, or several hours over time.

Venue: This activity is best learned at home, where you have tools and supplies. Once your children get the can-do attitude, they can do it anywhere, even when you're not there.

Equipment: Tool kit sufficient for the job, materials as needed.

Encourage Your Child to Decide What to Fix

Probably the most important advice we can give about this activity is "*Find the right task*"—fix something the child will enjoy fixing. The easiest way to determine what the activity should be is to wait until your child breaks something he or she really loves. But if that looks like a long wait, there are alternatives. You can suggest something, taking your child's interests and tastes into consideration. Many children have strong likes and dislikes when it comes to tasks. Kate, for example, loved mixing the cement for the basketball stand but hated screwing in all the little pieces needed to assemble a foosball table.

Things break and accidents happen, whether we like it or not, and we have to fix them! When I (Kate) spilled cranberry juice on an Oriental rug that had a lot of white in it, I was afraid I'd get in trouble. But my mother just said, "Let's see what we can do. It's not the end of the world, but we *do* need to get this up. I'll teach you something my mother taught me." I enjoyed the feeling of something being passed on from my grandmother to my mother to me. My mother asked me to get a white cloth and some club soda, and then we worked on removing the stain together. She showed me how to pour on the club soda, dab at it with a clean cloth—"Don't rub it, just gently dab it until it soaks it up—you don't want to rub it around and spread it, just have it get soaked up through the clean rag." My mother did one half; I did the other, asking questions and getting feedback like "You can use a little more pressure—how could you get that pressure?" I figured out that I could put the rag on the stain and just stomp on it with my feet, and my mother said, "Good thinking!"

Teach your children how to accomplish a new task by first showing them how to do it, and then letting them try it on their own. Learning to fix things with you encourages your children to be more resourceful and, later, they can try to fix something by themselves without needing to be shown first.

> Learning to fix things with you encourages your children to be more resourceful and, later, they can try to fix something by themselves without needing to be shown first.

Finding the right time is as important as finding the right object. Fiona, the woman whose headmaster made sure no one graduated from Concord Academy without knowing how to fix a flat tire, remembers the time her 10-year-old son Charles had a friend over and a window got broken:

I'm not sure if he broke the window or his friend did—I know he was concerned about how to explain it, because he didn't want to seem to be passing the blame to his friend. At any rate, we agreed that "these things happen" and, after the friend went home, Charles and I decided to fix the window, even though neither one of us had ever done that before and didn't know how.

Waiting until the friend had gone home was a good idea. If Fiona had made her son take care of the window while the friend was still there, it would have been hard for him to concentrate. Fiona's matter-of-fact attitude was also helpful; when a child breaks something, avoid the two extremes of anger ("You're so clumsy!") and overacceptance ("It's OK, honey, we can buy a new one"). You as a parent need to assign responsibility, but you can do that without hurting your child's feelings.

Fixing things shows the child that the consequences of mistakes can be corrected. Even if you can't fix the actual object (shattered crystal) you can usually do something to lessen the loss. Letting children get away with breaking things encourages them to be irresponsible and passive. Kids need not cry if they spill milk, but they should clean it up.

Be safe. Your child may want to fix a defective electrical outlet, a broken gas furnace, or sagging gutters two stories high. However, you must judge if the task is too dangerous or if it would require a level of knowledge or skill too great for your child.

Research How to Fix It

Part of the fun of fixing things is figuring out how to do it, whether through research or a friend's advice. One mother remembers:

> When Miranda was about six, she got some bubblegum in her hair. She had heard of kids getting gum in their hair and their mothers cutting the hair to get it out. When she showed me, her first comment was "I don't care if I have bubblegum in my hair—you can't cut it! I don't mind having gum in my hair!"

"Well, maybe there's something else we can do. What can we do to find more information?"

"Look on the Web!"

"Good idea. What should we type?"

"Bubblegum hair."

So we did and they said to use peanut butter!

Apply peanut butter to the area affected, gently rubbing it into the gum. The peanut butter will loosen and slightly dissolve the gum.

We did and it worked.

You can also encourage your child to use books: "Maybe *The Joy of Cooking* has something on that" or "What other books may have something on this topic?" You can persuade your child to think of other ways to find this information, such as calling a friend, a relative, or an expert.

Fiona believes that "If you take the trouble to analyze and understand a problem, you can figure it out." So here's what she and 10-year-old Charles did when they decided to fix the window:

We analyzed the situation: we started by pulling the broken glass out—and putting it in a thick bag so the garbage men wouldn't hurt themselves. As we did that, we could see that the glass was held in by little metal triangles, and that they were embedded in hard, cracked stuff, painted on the outside and white on the inside.

"How do you suppose that was put in here?" I asked, and Charles said that it must have once been soft because it was sticking exactly to everything and looked as if it had been spread in there like peanut butter.

So we put the little metal things and the white stuff in another bag and decided to take it with us to the hardware store. I asked Charles what we should do next before going to the store. After brainstorming some ideas, he thought to measure the window pane. He wrote down the measurements, and then we went to the hardware store.

"I know exactly what you need," the man said. He told us that the little triangles were called "glazier's points" and that the other stuff was putty. When we felt the putty, it was soft, like pudding. We were perplexed—we didn't understand how to put the glazier's points into it, and he told us we needed a putty knife.

We did what he told us to do, and Charles made notes:

1. Put the glass in. (They cut it for us at the hardware store, using Charles's measurements.)

2. Put the points in. I held the glass in place while Charles stuck the points in the wood and pressed them in place with the edge of the knife.

How to Fix the Window
① Put glass in
② Put points in
③ Spread putty around

3. Spread the putty around. The really great thing about putty that we discovered is that it feels fun—like soft clay!

It wasn't really that hard to fix the window, though it sounded hard until Fiona explained how she and her son figured it out and then carried out what they had learned. When we asked her what advice she had for other parents, she said:

Teach your kids to think it through, because things take on an out-of-proportion difficulty if you don't. Remember that very young kids have a short attention span; you shouldn't spoil the fun of the activity by tying them down to it, forcing them to finish it.

We agree—but we also think that it's important to show kids that they *can* fix things and let them have the satisfaction of seeing the tangible results. Encouraging kids 10 and older to persevere can result in their learning to achieve while surmounting obstacles. There is a huge sense of accomplishment when you finish something, even though you may not *want* to finish it. Think of a trainer at the gym getting you to do more push-ups; you're always glad you did them afterwards.

It's OK to *coax* a child to finish ("Can we give it five more minutes?"), but not to *force* a child to finish. For really long, hard jobs (like assembling something really complicated), you can also give them the option of finishing later: "How about if we do the rest tomorrow?"

Use what you know about your child to be flexible. You're not necessarily stifling his or her resourcefulness, if you are the one who ends up actually completing the task. Your child will still learn.

I (Kate) recall when my mother showed me how to get the cranberry juice off the carpet, we got most of it off with the clean cloth and club soda together. But my mother cleaned the rest of the stain out with a commercial stain remover because I was too young at the time to handle chemicals. But I still learned how to do it, and remembered it as something fun my mother had taught me, not a chore—and the attitude and approach stayed with me, too.

> It's OK to *coax* a child to finish, but not to *force* a child to finish.

People who are good at fixing things tend to be confident, competent, creative, persevering, and independent. If you don't raise the kind of child who can repair a broken fan belt, don't fret. If you do the activities in this chapter repeatedly, your child will gradually learn that when something breaks it's worth trying to fix it, and that the trying alone can be rewarding. With repeated successes, children will understand that when something breaks, they *can* probably figure out how to fix it—and that will make them both more confident and more resourceful.

CHAPTER 8

LEARN TO DISCIPLINE YOURSELF

At last, however, the master sent a note to my father, asking why I was not sent to school. When my father read this note, he called me up, and I knew very well I was in the devil of a hobble, for my father had been taking a few horns [of whisky], and was in a good condition to make the fur fly. He called on me to know why I had not been in school. I told him I was afraid to go, and that the master would whip me .... but I soon found that I was not to expect a better fate at home, for my father told me, in a very angry manner, that he would whip me an eternal sight worse than the master, if I didn't start immediately to the school.

—*David Crockett,* A Narrative of the Life of David Crockett[1]

N FRONTIER TIMES AND INTO THE 1950s and 1960s, most American parents handled discipline the way Davy Crockett's father did. Today, parents may be more likely to behave in the opposite (and, in our view, equally ineffective) extreme: either they can be too lenient or ignore problems. But no matter how parents discipline them, children will do things they shouldn't do. Smart Parenting techniques lessen behavior problems because kids become their own disciplinarians.

This chapter discusses different approaches parents can take to prevent and correct their children's behavioral problems. Even when your child has done something seriously wrong, if you remain calm and take the time to think about it, you can figure out a response that will help your child in that particular situation and help prevent recurrences, too. We recommend these basic steps:

- Get the facts and then decide—calmly and rationally—what you're going to do.

- Talk about the whole situation with your child, including the punishment and preventive measures, and make your child a key decision maker in the process.

- Follow through on whatever you decide.

What you say and do will depend on you, your child, and the situation, but these steps will usually be appropriate. There is one principle that always applies: focus on the *behavior* and *talk about bad behavior, not a bad child*. Convey the attitude that you disapprove of what the child did, but that you still love the child. Telling a child that you disapprove of *her* or that *she* is a bad person, fills her with shame and teaches her that she is worthless. People can change how they act, but they can't instantly change who they are. If you only take one suggestion from this chapter, let it be to criticize the behavior, not the child. That's easy to say, but for some parents, hard to do: we give examples that we hope will help.

> If you only take one suggestion from this chapter, let it be to criticize the behavior, not the child.

Get All the Facts, Then Decide What to Do

Some situations don't require much parental detective work or decision making. When, for example, I (Kate) accidentally pulled all the fur off my brother's gerbil's tail, and then panicked and hid the furry tube in the cedar chips, it was easy for my mother to get the facts (she asked me what happened to the gerbil's tail) and deal with the situation immediately. She told me that she knew I hadn't meant to hurt the gerbil, but that it *was* wrong to have been sneaky about it.

Together, we asked Geoff to demonstrate the proper tail-holding procedure.

Sometimes situations are more complicated and parents need to play detective or think hard to decide how to handle the circumstance in the way that will help their child most. Use your knowledge of your child and consider the seriousness of the situation when talking about your child's behavior with him or her. There are times when a direct confrontation isn't the best solution.

In high school, Erin (a client) had to give a short speech in history. She didn't want to use note cards, so she wrote notes on her hands. She kept her hands folded and glanced down at them when she needed a cue, sort of like using a teleprompter. Her history teacher noticed her looking at her hands and suggested using note cards instead. But when she was in science class, taking a test, the science teacher pointed to Erin's hands and asked, "What's this?" "Oh, don't worry—it's not for this class," she responded. The teacher assumed Erin cheated by writing science notes on her hands.

That afternoon, unbeknownst to Erin, the science teacher called her parents, telling them that Erin had cheated. The teacher went on to say that she didn't "think this needs to be dealt with by the school, but ...." Her parents discussed the event that afternoon.

They knew Erin was under a lot of pressure since she had just started at a new school. She was meeting all new people, taking classes that were more advanced than she had taken in her previous school, and was trying hard in a lot of areas. They also knew that she really needed their support just then—and their good opinion and approval, too. They were hesitant to confront her directly, fearing it would just add to the pressure. But they also knew that they had to do something; they couldn't condone cheating! Erin's parents weren't afraid to be strict and confront their children: they'd done it before, but in this situation they just knew a direct confrontation wasn't the way to go.

Erin's parents calmly asked, "What happened with the notes on your hands?" But they didn't make any accusations. Had they screamed, "Your science teacher caught you cheating! Haven't we taught you to be honest?" Erin would have been defensive and shouted back that she hadn't cheated, that the notes on her hands were for a speech, and how dare they accuse her of such a thing? Making blunt accusations is poor detective work. Her parents' calm, non-confrontational approach got out the facts. Erin called her science teacher and said, "You didn't check my hands, but my history teacher did and you can call him and see that I didn't cheat." Her parents' calm detective work disclosed that she hadn't cheated and, of course, no discipline was necessary.

> **Making blunt accusations is poor detective work.**

A client remembers a friend being given a hatchet when he was about seven—and being so thrilled with it that he hacked down a dozen small trees on his parents' property. When he looked around and saw the trail of gashes behind him, he knew he'd done something bad and ran to his father, "Someone's been following me around, cutting down trees!" His father just looked at him, smiling in such a kind, understanding way that the child knew his father knew he was lying. But this father never said anything at all and the child, who felt ashamed of himself, was left with the feeling that it was OK to lie and to destroy other people's property.

We'd like to report that he grew out of this feeling, but unfortunately, he never did. In fact, he became one of the most manipulative, deceitful men our client ever knew! The parents believed no discipline was best and never imposed consequences for misbehavior. The parents weren't interested in "getting all the facts" about their son's misbehavior. They didn't care about the truth, ethics, or honesty—and their child grew up to have poor values.

Your knowledge of your child and the situation will guide you to the best solution—if you take the time to analyze all of the factors. The key is to get all the facts, deal with your emotions about them, and then decide rationally about what kind of discussion would be most helpful to have with your child, while avoiding the following two extremes:

1. Reacting too harshly or hysterically makes children exceedingly fearful of the pending consequences and you. They become afraid to even let you find out what they've done, let alone discuss it with you. This could lead to lying, cheating, sneakiness, and,

worst of all, a pattern of denial—of dealing with difficulties by running away from them.

2. Reacting too leniently or, worse, just ignoring the whole issue makes children think you don't care. It teaches them that their actions have no consequences or that it's OK to do things that are wrong.

Both reactions are harmful to the child. Take the time to think about it and find the right balance.

Sometimes, you may find out what your child has done from someone else and you have plenty of time in private to decide what to do about it. You might even have time to discuss it with others. But there are times that you may have to make a spot decision. However, even if you are face to face with your child when you find out that he or she has done something awful, you can still usually take a little time for yourself: "I need to think about this and calm down before we talk." Calmly discussing what happened and figuring out appropriate discipline and preventive measures teaches children to handle problems rationally. It models the way you want your child to think and act, in the present and in the future.

Talk About It with Your Child

When I (Kate) accidentally pulled off the gerbil's tail, my parents knew that the fur would grow back, so "no harm done." But, I had made two mistakes: lifting the gerbil by the tail improperly and hiding the evidence in the cedar ships. The most important discussion concerned owning up to mistakes, telling the truth, and being strong enough to experience consequences.

Moral development is limited by age; few eight-year-olds can grasp the concept of "social contract" (you don't steal from me and I won't steal from you) and how societies advance. Yet even four-year-olds can learn rules—rules they must follow so as not to disappoint their parents or hurt others. An approach that many parents use in discussing misbehavior with young children is based on the Golden Rule; they ask, "How would you feel if someone did that to you?" The question is intended to elicit the answer, "Not very good."

Discussion with preteens and teenagers should take a more serious tone, conveying the message, "Your character is being formed, so we as parents must instill moral values." Even eight-year-olds can grasp how their lives will be damaged if they continue stealing, being destructive, or lying.

The calm but serious discussion must lead to consequences now. The ideal is for the child to impose the consequences on himself or herself. After my (Kate's) mom calmly got out the facts, she asked, "Kate, what should you do?" Looking at the tail-less gerbil, I felt awful, and I said, "I'll apologize to Geoff and buy him a new gerbil." Geoff appreciated the apology after he blew up, but I learned I could take the punishment, and, most important, I could figure out my own discipline.

> **Most important, I could figure out my own discipline.**

At times, however, this might not be enough. There are times when parents need to confront their children—and pretty severely and directly when something serious has happened.

Parents who try to be buddies with their children without firm, agreed-upon rules have trouble establishing limits and applying discipline after serious misbehavior. But even if it's hard to do this, they should try! We understand that many parents want to be friends with their children and we agree that parents and children should like and trust each other. But parents have a legal and moral obligation to pull rank when necessary. No matter how friendly you and your child are, it's not—and it shouldn't be—a peer relationship, because you must exercise authority, in the best interest of your child. Your children need that authority—especially when they have misbehaved.

Parents who are authoritarian, constantly imposing and giving orders and reacting harshly to small infractions, can make misbehavior even worse. They may be out of touch with their children or open communication may have broken down completely. For these parents, a crisis can be an opportunity. The child's misbehavior may even be a cry for help. Parents can use the crisis as an opportunity to loosen up a little and, while still retaining some authority, listen to their child and include him or her in the process of figuring out what to do.

The following conversation could almost be a perfect script for handling really serious misbehavior. It's long, but we think you'll find it worth reading. When a neighbor's child, Jason, was about 10, he joined a wild friend, Brian, in pelting another neighbor's new Mercedes with rocks, almost causing an accident. This was definitely a time for tough talk, backed up by action from the parents. Here's what took place, and it's an excellent example of the Smart Parenting approach to discipline:[2]

Father: I can't believe it—rocks tossed at Mrs. Jones' Mercedes!

Jason: It was Brian's idea.

Father: I see. A serious accident could have resulted—and it's all Brian's fault?

Jason: It was really dumb. I wasn't thinking.

Father: Suppose when Mrs. Jones jerked her car to the left, she hit a van with ten kids in it, and just suppose three kids and Mrs. Jones were now dead and seven others were hospitalized. Suppose all their families were in the room here, now. What would you say to them?

Jason: I'll never, ever do anything like that again.

Father: Jason, if all those family members of the dead and injured were here, now, how would you feel and how do you think *I* would feel?

Jason: You would be mad at me.

Father: That's not good enough. "Mr. Jones, sorry your wife is dead, but I just want you to know I'm really mad at Jason." Try again. What feelings would I have in addition to anger?

Jason: You'd be sad. Embarrassed. Scared. Everyone would hate me and you.

Father: They'd hate me because ... what?

Jason: You didn't teach me right from wrong.

Father: Right. OK, we've gotten out your feelings and mine and Mrs. Jones'. Now tell me all the details of what happened. ...

Jason: ... (related to the details)

Father: Next, please tell me what sort of consequences, punishment, discipline would be appropriate for you.

Jason: A lot.

Father: What's the goal?

Jason: To punish me for being bad.

Father: Wrong. Jason, you didn't kill or hurt anyone. What is most important to you, me, your mom, Mrs. Jones, and all the kids and all the parents who might be really hurt next time?

Jason: There won't be a next time.

Father: Good! That's the goal! So you figure it out, the punishment that would guarantee you won't do things in the future that hurt people's property and could hurt people.

Jason: You want me to tell you what my punishment will be?

Father: You're darned right. If I'm not going to hold your hand and think for you in the future, I'm not the best person to say how your goal should be achieved. Of course, we could ask Brian to create your punishment, because he's good at thinking for you!

Jason: No way! He's an idiot. I acted like one too. I just didn't think.

Father: Not thinking is serious, Jason. You are capable of good thinking that will result in smart choices and good behaviors. You've done well for ten years, until today, so it's important to figure out what to do to prevent a recurrence. Let's get your plan started. I'll write. What do you need to do?

Jason: Apologize.

Father: To whom?

Jason: To Mrs. Jones.

Father: and ...?

Jason: ... to you as my parents. I'm really sorry.

Father: Thank you. And what will you say to Mrs. Jones?

Jason: I'm really sorry and it'll never happen again.

Father: You're sorry because …?

Jason: Because I didn't think, and the rocks could have caused her to run into another car and people could have been killed, or I could have really damaged her car.

Father: What would help you to really think through all of the reasons why you're sorry and what you should have done when Brian suggested throwing rocks?

Jason: Write it out?

Father: Good idea. … You can do a 500-word paper tonight and give it to Mrs. Jones, and mom and me tomorrow. Brian's parents should see it, too. OK, your punishment plan will include apologizing to Mrs. Jones and writing the paper. What else?

Jason: I don't know.

Father: What needs fixing?

Jason: Mrs. Jones' car.

Father: Her brand-new Mercedes. That could be very expensive.

Jason: I'll pay for it. I mow lawns for spending money, and I could offer to mow Jones' lawn until the damage is paid for.

Father: That could mean a full day per week all summer or two half days. How will you make the time?

Jason: I'll have to give up either baseball or swimming.

Father: Good for you. You love both sports, but giving one up is a consequence of your misbehavior. What else? What are you going to tell Brian the next time the two of you are together?

Jason: I'll tell him everything we've talked about and he'll never get me to do something like that again.

As Jason said years later, "A good spanking would have been easier on me. Having to think up consequences, disappointing my parents, apologizing, and working all summer—that's tough! I guess it made me think hard before doing something like that."

Jason never seriously misbehaved again, even during his teens. Jason's parents achieved their goal because they talked with him rationally about what had happened—they were tough but rational.

However you talk with your child, we urge you to *handle the situation in a rational way, because that's what allows the child's rational thinking to develop*. If you scream and yell and react impatiently, what you're teaching your kid is that this is the way problems are handled, instead of showing them how to think and figure out good solutions.

Let's repeat: Jason never seriously misbehaved again. His parents instilled self-discipline using a variety of Smart Parenting techniques. When children thoughtfully impose harsh disciplinary action on themselves, the learning is positive and long-lasting. Contrast that with the mutual screaming, name calling, and grounding punishments, when kids become motivated to misbehave even more to spite their parents.

> Handle the situation in a rational way, because that's what allows the child's rational thinking to develop.

If a child simply does not come up with a disciplinary plan, parents must dictate it. Here's an example.

When she was five or six, a friend, Sophie, was visiting her grandmother overnight. She loved her grandmother very much. But one afternoon, she looked through her grandmother's drawers and found a beautiful gold pocket watch. It was so smooth, and shiny, and golden that she had to have it. She packed it in her suitcase and took it home. But later she felt awful about stealing it and, after awhile, she couldn't stand it.

> When children thoughtfully impose harsh disciplinary action on themselves, the learning is positive and long-lasting.

She brought the watch to her mother and said, "Look what I found behind my bed! It must be a treasure from a long time ago."

"I don't think you just found this, did you?" her mother said, seriously, but gently.

"I did, I did! It's probably a pirate treasure."

Her mother just looked at her, raised one eyebrow, and asked, "Are you sure?"

"No, I took it from Grandma's," Sophie said, and started to cry. She told her mother what had happened. Her mother told her father. Then both of them talked with Sophie.

"You can't just take things that aren't yours." Sophie's father said. "What you did was stealing. It was Grandpa's watch." Her parents asked her what she should do, but young Sophie kept saying, "I don't know." So, they said she had to call her grandmother, confess, and apologize. She begged to be given another punishment instead: "I'll clean the whole house! Please, don't make me tell Grandma!" Her parents were adamant.

Luckily (or so it seemed to Sophie, who later found out that her parents had called her grandmother first, to prepare her), her grandmother reacted beautifully. Her grandmother listened, and then said, "You can give it back to me the next time you come visit—and you can borrow the watch anytime you want to. Just ask me first. You should never take another person's things without asking, even if that person is family."

Then they talked about other things. By the time she hung up the phone, Sophie knew that, although she had done something wrong, her grandmother still loved her just as much as before. Sophie's parents and grandmother handled the situation in a way that was right for her and reflected the seriousness of Sophie's actions. When she told us this story, Sophie ended by saying she never stole anything from anyone ever again.

Follow Through: Deal with the Consequences and Take Preventive Measures

Talking the situation over with your child is only the first step: parents need to follow through with action. They lose integrity and their children's respect if they don't follow through on the agreed-upon punishment.

Many parents take the easy way out by not following through. They ignore the whole incident after the initial confrontation or conversation, which shows the children that their behavior has no real consequence or that their parents don't keep their promises. It encourages children to not trust their parents and, indirectly, not to trust themselves: "If my parents don't do what they say they will do, why should I?" It can also make children think that they're not important enough, or the situation isn't important enough, for their parents to remember it or follow through on it. So if, for example, your child is to write a 500-word paper as a punishment that day, insist on seeing it before he goes to bed.

Punishments are one way to prevent recurrences; incentives are another. When children are older, the right incentives can really help prevent kids from making huge mistakes, especially about those things that can ruin young lives, such as car accidents.

> Punishments are one way to prevent recurrences; incentives are another.

The Smarts and some other families made driving contracts with their children that began this way: "At 16 years of age, you'll get your driver's license and drive your mom's SUV, because it's big and safe. If you do not cause a serious accident and if you do not have a moving violation more than five miles an hour over the speed limit, then after one year we'll buy you a used car. When you go off to college, you keep the car and that contract expires, but by then you'll be totally responsible as a driver. If you violate even one of the conditions, you don't get to drive the car." For most kids a car means freedom and peer approval. When that powerful positive incentive is reinforced by an equally powerful negative incentive—the loss of that car—you can prevent poor judgment from ruining or even ending a young life. We think that's a pretty powerful incentive for parents.

Geoff and Kate never violated the contract, made it through the first year of driving when most kids have accidents, and have retained their safe driving habits (and records) ever since. The small print to the contract permitted fender benders, "but you have to pay for the repairs." For moving violations less than five miles per hour, "you pay the fine, that's all."

<u>CAR CONTRACT</u>
1991

I Get to Use the Car, With the Following
Consequences:

1. No penalty for speeding ticket(s) less than
   3.5 mph over Speed limit
2. I pay 100% of fines
3. I pay all increases in insurance as a result
   of traffic violations / accidents
4. If I cause accident(s) I pay for repairs
   and lose driving privileges for 1 year after
   1 major accident or 2 minor accidents

_____   _____
name   date
Katy Smart   May, 1991

There is another reason for having consequences: discipline reinforces moral values such as honesty. Raising children who grow up to be deeply happy adults means raising children with strong moral values, because people without a moral compass are rarely truly happy.

> Discipline reinforces moral values such as honesty.

We believe that most people are hardwired for honesty early in life. It's never too early to talk about, encourage, and, most important of all, demonstrate the importance of honesty and other moral values. Probably the most powerful way to prevent kids from misbehaving is to set a good example and then reinforce it with discipline, ideally punitive consequences they impose on themselves. Resourcefulness can be guided ethically and morally—or not. If you live your life with integrity and you discipline your children wisely and consistently, they will have a moral compass to guide them through life.

Notes

1. David Crockett, *A Narrative of the Life of David Crockett.* Reprint edition. Lincoln: University of Nebraska Press, 1986.

2. Names have been changed and permissions obtained to report this case study.

CHAPTER 9

ENJOY WEEKENDS AWAY!

"I have often been asked how I came to write Swallows *and* Amazons. *The answer is that it had its beginning long, long ago when, as children, my brother, sisters and I spent most of our holidays on a farm at the south end of Coniston [in England]. We played in or on the lake or on the hills above it, finding friends in the farmers and shepherds and charcoal burners whose smoke rose from the woods along the shore. We adored the place. Coming to it, we used to run down to the lake, dip our hands in, and make wishes. Going away from it, we were in tears. While away from it, as children and grown-ups, we dreamt about it. No matter where I was, wandering about the world, I used at night to look for the North Star and, in my mind's eye, could see the beloved skyline of great hills beneath it."*

—*Arthur Ransome, Author's Note,* Swallows and Amazons[1]

THOUSANDS OF THE SUCCESSFUL PEOPLE we interviewed have expressed similar feelings. The words may not be as poetic, but their appreciation for a country place, a change from their ordinary lives, is just as deep. This chapter shows the impact that regularly visiting a beloved place can have on your children.

Both the beauty of the place and the kind of experiences children can have there can benefit kids. Most of the high achievers we interviewed who had spent summers and weekends in the country (usually in a modest cabin or camping out) said that these experiences, more than anything else in their childhoods, had contributed to their resourcefulness—to their love of life, creativity, can-do attitude, and problem solving. They also discovered talents they never knew they had and formed new interests that sometimes lasted a lifetime. Being in a different place afforded them greater freedom, enabling them to do different things and even be different people than they could be at home.

A country visit can provide practice at adapting to new situations and problem solving. As one parent put it, "There may be more possibilities for adventure in the country than in the city or suburbs." Your children's daily lives may be super structured or very supervised, perhaps because in many places it really isn't safe for children to roam around without an adult. If that is the case, rural life can be liberating for the whole family.

This chapter explains:

■ Why it's valuable to get away with your family, with examples from summers and weekends we spent at our cabin and from what parents we interviewed told us about their trips.

> A country visit can provide practice at adapting to new situations and problem solving.

■ How you can use a weekend cabin (or camper or tent) to give your family experiences none of you could have at home, and how those experiences build resourcefulness.

It's Good for a Family to Get Away

The most obvious benefit of getting away is the freedom it gives the whole family. More unstructured time in a safe environment means children can play and explore and do projects or just enjoy doing nothing! And they can do a lot on their own. A cabin is the perfect setting for almost any activity in this book.

Getting away fosters a positive cycle of trying new things, becoming more resourceful, and becoming more curious; exploring and making discoveries on their own is just plain fun! A child can have a ball doing something as simple as chasing frogs or spying on a turtle.

I (Kate) remember one of my early adventures with my friend Jamie, whom we had invited along to the cabin for the weekend. I recall that it was late fall, way too cold to go swimming, and we decided that we were going to put on hip boots or waders and go tromping through the lake—being in the deep cold water without getting even a *little* bit wet was really fun. It was also interesting to be in water up to our hips and not get wet at all! We saw cattails (tall, reedy marsh plants that are brown and fuzzy at the top—and felt furry too when we touched them) and weeds that came up looking like straws.

As we walked, the mud got thicker and more glue-like—it got so thick that we could lean backwards and not fall over; the mud held us up. It felt like we were defying gravity. We were doing that and laughing—and then when we tried to walk away, we couldn't. We'd sunk in the mud and were stuck. Muck had molded around our boots like cement. We couldn't move at all.

Our first reaction was panic. It was cold, we couldn't move, and the sun was going down, so we started screaming. We shouted for help for what seemed like a long time, and finally my dad came out. He laughed and yelled, "You can figure it out and I'll make hot chocolate!" At first we complained, "Save us!" but then concluded that we had to do something ourselves. We decided to get out of our hip boots, swim through the sludge, and run back to the cabin in our socks. Jamie was worried that we'd get in trouble for leaving the hip boots: "I'm sure they cost a lot of money," she said, but I said that we could come back and get them later: "We can use planks, or get them next year when it thaws—our lives are more important than hip boots!"

We wriggled out of them and jumped into the sludgy, muddy water—it was really cold and really thick. We used our arms to half-swim and half-run through it.

By the time we got back to the cabin, our adrenaline was pumping so hard we felt like we had sky dived out of an airplane or something. My father was—or seemed—suitably impressed. When we told him we'd left the waders behind, he said, "Good for you! That was the right thing to do. I'm proud of you for figuring it out." And as we warmed up by the fireplace and drank hot chocolate, we felt proud of ourselves, too. In retrospect, Jamie and I felt defeated until my dad gave us the ultimate but very basic Smart Parenting challenge: figure it out!

> The ultimate but very basic Smart Parenting challenge: figure it out!

Cabins are for high adventure and activity, not for fancy clothes or magazine-worthy home décor. Kids from the city arrived at our cabin squeaky-clean, in pressed jeans, expecting to be entertained, but went home a little messier and a lot more excited. Parents reported to us that their children raved about how much fun it had been to learn how to build fires, shoot a bow and arrow, parasail, clear paths in the woods with hatchets like pioneers, and do other things they never did at home. They also met people they didn't meet at home. (This is also a reason to revisit the same place: your children's friendships can develop in ways that they couldn't if you went to a different place each time.) People who grew up with a summer cabin often talk about the friends they made there.

When our friend Emily went to northern Minnesota as a girl, she joined the local water ski team and met a girl named Gina. "Gina was really poor," she told us. "Their house didn't even have a front door, just a board that you pulled up. The whole place was probably about 400 square feet, you spent the night in sweats and wool socks and lots of blankets and quilts because there wasn't much heat, and old towels covered the windows." This wasn't like visiting someone from her suburban high school! It made Emily more open-minded and she became, as she put it herself, "a more real person—and a lot less superficial, catty, and materialistic."

People often say foreign travel broadens the mind. Getting to know people from different cultural backgrounds in your own country can also be broadening and beneficial. If you choose a place where people live differently than you do, and you go back to it year after year, so your children's friendships have a chance to grow, your kids can gain a deep understanding of other people's lives and values.

There are other benefits to these friendships. If your cabin is in a rural area, your kids will develop friendships with kids accustomed to working hard, taking responsibility, making their own fun, and figuring out all kinds of things on their own.

Be Prepared ... for Lots of Fun!

The most important preparation is the location of the cabin, tent, or trailer. Choose one that's different from home—not a resort or anything else that duplicates your life in a different setting. For most of us, this means someplace rural. If you live in the country, try weekends in the city!

We also suggest renting a place that's within weekend driving (rather than flying) distance: you'll get there more often and it's not *so* remote that there aren't many other people there. A cabin on a lake or a river provides unlimited possibilities for fun, family bonding, and learning. Paddle around any lake in the United States on the 4th of July and you'll see families enjoying picnics, kids playing all sorts of sports they've organized, and kids figuring things out—from how to pitch a tent to how to resolve a dispute with another kid.

Kate and Geoff had plenty of chores to do at the cabin, but instead of complaining, they figured out ways to make the tasks more fun, by either singing or making up talking games during that time. Chores were not typically seen as a burden, but rather tasks that needed to get done and were a way to help out. To encourage resourcefulness, we assigned them tasks, but encouraged them to figure out efficient ways to do them. For example, when they had to paint a shed, Kate and Geoff asked around and a neighbor helped them learn to use a spray gun. They were finished by mid-morning and we complimented them on their productivity and efficiency. "Way to go! Have fun the rest of the day!"

Parents, be prepared to flex and learn! It takes kids about two days to suggest a hundred activities. They'll want to ride horses, bring pet frogs into the house, trap squirrels, build ant colonies, sneak up on a deer, plant gardens—and guess what? You parents will have to figure out if you want to observe, ignore, coach, or master the many responsibilities.

Make the transition easier by not sweating the small stuff, like dirty clothes. When the kids run around in the rain and mud, be happy for them and just wash the clothes. Or for older kids, have them do the washing. Parents aren't maids or slaves. At the cabin, the kids join in to cook, clean, and do chores, and their reward is more fun than they typically have back home. Furniture should be durable, and who cares if there are nicks and scrapes on any of it? By the way, kids are durable and they learn not to sweat nicks and scrapes on themselves either!

> Make the transition easier by not sweating the small stuff.

A client, Thomas, remembers his parents announcing that they were going to spend a summer on a cabin on Lake Shasta, in northern California. He remembers thinking that he'd be "trapped with my parents and no friends" and brought a big suitcase of books and comic books. Although he ended up figuring out other ways to have fun too, the books gave him a way to entertain himself right away. Eventually his curiosity pulled him outside and he met kids, made friends, and learned new sports, how to build and fix things, and how to get along with kids different from those back home. But years later, he also recalls the pure serenity of curling up with a book, under a tree.

Set Ground Rules with a Purpose

Everyone we talk with agrees on the importance of this rule: no more than one hour each day with TV, DVDs, computer games, iPods, or anything else that requires a headset. Your children may initially complain about this, but within a day or so they learn to explore and make their own fun. Soon they won't miss the electronics. As Thomas, the boy on Lake Shasta (which is where the family decided to spend time every summer), said, "At home, TV was a divisive thing: my father was downstairs watching something no one else wanted to watch, my mother was reading someplace, and we were in our rooms doing different things. On the houseboat after dinner we played cards or Parcheesi—something we could all play together. Kids always want someone to play with them, and it was fun to be *doing* something."

A well-documented example of the make-your-own-entertainment rule (and the benefits of rural living as a break) comes from the PBS documentary *Frontier House,* in which three American families lived as pioneers in rural Montana in 1883. They lived exactly the way the pioneers did (everything was as it was then, including the underwear and outhouses), except that cameras recorded their words and activities. In an early interview, one of the children was asked what he would miss. He said, "I'll miss my room, my TV, my Nintendo, my Nintendo 64, my cell phone," and a long list of other electronic games.

After awhile, he was asked what he'd discovered. He said that he did things there he would have thought were "kind of stupid at home—like make bows and arrows and play with them. But here it's fun. I guess you could say ..." He paused, obviously thinking, and then his whole face lit up as he said, "I guess you could say I've discovered imagination."

His sister said, "I thought I'd never survive without my TV and my radio, and that I'd have to get someone to tape all my shows—but I don't need them, I don't miss them. It's more fun to just hang out here!" And she cried when it was time to leave: "If they don't let me keep Snowball [her horse], I don't know what I'll do." She had discovered that she had a real talent for taking care of animals; in fact, she ended up being the go-to person for the whole community whenever anything was wrong with an animal. She decided to become a vet. But that isn't the point. The point is that she discovered a gift she'd never known she had.

Until I (Kate) was about 10, I disliked reading. However, at the cabin, I (like Thomas at Lake Shasta) discovered the joys of quiet time reading a good book—in front of the fire, in my tree house, or on my bed. People we surveyed said during weekends away they'd discovered:

- A lifelong love of astronomy
- A talent for square dancing (still a Saturday night local tradition in western Massachusetts)
- Passions for collecting (and, in some cases, then reading about)

rocks, fossils, caterpillars, birds, etc.

- The excitement of speed—dirt bikes, motorcycles, ATVs, snow-mobiles, etc.
- Things that fly—kits, toy planes, rockets, etc.
- Tracking animals—all kinds of animals!
- How to be alone, but happy
- Chopping wood
- Catching frogs, tadpoles, minnows, butterflies, squirrels, etc.
- Hunting and fishing
- How to build and fix things
- Needlepoint
- Changing the spark plugs on snowmobiles and ATVs
- Reading for fun
- Writing for fun
- The joy of watching campfires
- Figuring out how to tow cars with a tractor

Who knows what your children will discover? When they're left to find interests for themselves and can pursue those interests in their own ways, it's hard to predict what will fascinate children.

Some parents don't organize any activities: they just let their children run wild and explore on their own. The writer Colette, who grew up in the country, once wrote that her mother was happy *not* knowing where her children were during the day. She wanted them to be outside playing and exploring.[2]

If the idea of your children having that much freedom worries you a little, you can keep them "in range" enough to make sure they're safe and check on them occasionally. Some parents have minimal rules ("No going beyond the sound of the dinner bell" or "Be home before dark") and find delight in whatever their children do within the set boundaries, whether it's reading a classic novel on the porch or starting a tadpole collection or deciding to hack a trail with a hatchet. At the Smart cabin, the fire pit down by the water was a favorite place for teenagers to hang out at night. The pit was (and still is) 200 feet from the cabin, far enough away for kids to have a blast telling stories and roasting hot dogs, but close enough that parents could keep an eye on the activities.

Don't overschedule kids; the cabin can be a wonderful place for kids to go off and organize group activities on their own. When kids organize their own softball, volleyball, hide-and-seek, paintball, etc. they learn to lead, prevent conflict, compromise, resolve conflicts, and so on. They have to learn to get along with others and play fair without parents, coaches, and referees interceding. It's good for kids to learn to both lead—to motivate, encourage, and coach each other—and to follow—to be a team player. It's also a valuable lesson when cheaters are shunned. Kids can figure our how to put up the volleyball net and how to take it down and put it away correctly so that it's not so tangled up the next time. It's beneficial for older kids, who eventually can go water-skiing without parents, to learn to take responsibility for driving safely, resolving who will ski first, persuading kids not to do things too risky, and figuring out things like how to start a stalled engine. It's not just the location, but also the large amount of free time (unlike overscheduled time at home) that makes activities like this easier to initiate and learn from.

> The cabin can be a wonderful place for kids to go off and organize group activities on their own.

A balance of time alone and time together is usually most pleasant for everyone. We've noticed that when they relax, people fall into a pattern that suits them naturally and develop a family or house rhythm. Weekends away provide what everyone wants, because they choose how to fill the day. So most families find they can have individual time, kids' together time, and also family time for meals and board games. And this is a wonderful atmosphere for the blossoming of a can-do spirit.

Notes

1. Ransome, Arthur, *Swallows and Amazons*. Boston: David Godine Publisher, 1999. This series was first published in 1930 and has been read and loved by generations. As a recent reviewer said, it's "a perfect book

for anyone captivated by the world of adventure and imagination." We loved it when we were children and we love it now for the quality of the writing ("a perfect book," *as The Times Literary Supplement* said) and the fact that the young heroes and heroines are such can-do kids.

2. Colette (Sidonie-Gabrielle Colette), *Earthly Paradise*. London: Secker & Warburg, 1966.

CHAPTER 10

BE A NAVIGATOR

My mother was determined to make us independent. When I was four years old, she stopped the car a few miles from our house and made me find my own way home across the fields. I got hopelessly lost. My youngest sister Vanessa's earliest memory is being woken up in the dark one January morning because Mum had decided that I should cycle to Bournemouth that day. She packed some sandwiches and an apple and told me to find some water along the way. Bournemouth was fifty miles away from our home in Shamley Green, Surrey. I was under twelve, but Mum thought that it would teach me the importance of stamina and a sense of direction. I remember setting off in the dark, and I have a vague recollection of staying the night with a relative. I have no idea how I found their house, or how I got back to Shamley Green the next day, but I do remember finally walking back into the kitchen like a conquering hero, feeling tremendously proud of my marathon bike ride and expecting a huge welcome. "Well done, Ricky," Mum greeted me in the kitchen, where she was chopping onions. "Was that fun? Now, could you run along to the vicar's? He's got some logs he wants chopping and I told him that you'd be back any minute.

—Sir Richard Branson, founder, Virgin Group
(records, airlines, mobile phones, cola, etc.)[1]

I N THIS CHAPTER YOU WILL LEARN two separate activities to practice with your children that are included in what we call Navigator. One involves kids finding the way to a specific destination and the other has them planning an entire trip. Both versions of Navigator can be a very short, spontaneous activity that can be done as you're doing errands with your kids ("How do we get to the nearest drugstore?") or you can make it more challenging. ("How would you plan our vacation?")

It's frustrating and frightening to be lost, literally and metaphorically. Knowing how to get where you want to go—how to read a map, use a compass, ask for and follow directions—are skills that will give your child confidence, not just in the Navigator exercise but in life. People often talk about "life journeys" and "the joy is in the journey, not the arrival" and in this chapter, kids see how they can be in control of that journey.

Navigator builds resourcefulness, for it requires a clear goal (destination) and consideration of options (to get there).

Be a Navigator

Time: 15 minutes to several weeks, over time.

Venue: Any place except at home.

Equipment: Optional: map or compass.

You can perform the activities in this chapter with your children multiple times, raising the level of challenge as your children become older and more responsible. You can do it with a 4-year-old on the way to McDonald's or let an 18-year-old plan a long trip—it depends on your child and the complexity involved in getting to the destination.

Figure Out How to Get There

In Navigator, you don't need to do much preparation beyond picking a place, or encouraging your child to make that selection, as long as it fits the child's age and ability level. The most important thing is to allow enough time to get there—that is, enough time for mistakes and wrong turns. Don't engage in Navigator when you're in a rush to get to the doctor's office or late for the family picnic.

Young children might never have been asked to find their way any-where. Initially they may be intimidated by this activity. So we suggest starting with an easy destination—a place they want to go, like a friend's house—and then progressing to places that are harder to find. When a child wants to go somewhere in particular, you can introduce him or her to the game by saying, "OK, let's play a game called Navigator. That means that *you* guide us: you tell me every turn." When doing this with a very young child, you might say, "Let's pretend that I don't know how to get there, so you tell me." As you go, prompt your child with questions: "OK, an intersection is coming up—now what do I do?"

One benefit of the activity for very young children is that it intro-duces them to the kinds of things they have to pay attention to when finding their way somewhere—what to look at, how to read traffic sig-nals and signs. As a child, I (Kate) learned what yellow lights meant when my mother asked, "Do you know what the red, yellow, and green lights mean?" I remember knowing what the red and green lights stood for, but to my mother's chagrin, I said yellow meant "speed up."

You can present the exercise to your child as either playing a game that will be fun or trying an activity that will teach him or her something useful, or both. We do advise talking about it first and asking if your child wants to do it. If you just announce suddenly, "Now *you're* going to find our way to _____," your child may feel blindsided by the idea. If you just abruptly ask a question, he or she may feel that doing this is some kind of test. Introduce the idea and give him or her a choice about participating in the activity.

Choose a place your child wants to go that is a little challenging to find. Remember that something that comes easily and naturally to a parent may be very difficult for a young child. When young children are trying to find places, parents shouldn't get short or sarcastic, no matter how long it takes. If you can't be patient, don't do this activity!

You can begin playing Navigator with children as young as two or three, if you make the destination simple enough. I (Brad) found just such an opportunity with my three-year-old grandson, Will. When Will's parents were waiting for us in a big, crowded Rainforest Café® (a restaurant with a simulated jungle: trees, snakes, floor-to-ceiling fish tanks, wild animals, and rain), I suggested that he find the table by pretending he was exploring in the jungle. Will got quite excited at this idea, running all over the restaurant; but he couldn't find the table and started to get frustrated. So I said that I could get us to the table, but he should think of a way to find it without running. Without a word to me, Will grabbed the nearest waiter and said, "I'm Will Smart, can you find my parents?" The waiter checked the seating chart and, when he looked inquiringly at me, I quietly thanked him and explained that this was a learning game.

You can include several children in the activity. Two or three kids can, for example, work together to plot out your route—brainstorming, debating, correcting each other, and thinking of different ways to find directions or ask. You can make it all into a game by saying something like "Pretend I'm not from around here and I don't know, so you have to tell me. I'll only drive where you tell me to drive."

One father we know used his six-year-old daughter's desire to go to a toy store as the start of the game. He said he'd drive her there and buy her a small toy, if she could find the store. This kind of incentive isn't usually necessary, but some parents find it effective. This father was surprised at how well his daughter directed him. He also realized something else about his daughter—that she didn't know her left from her right.

The game doesn't have to involve driving or your own neighborhood: children who are old enough to read can navigate to other kinds of destinations, such as the subway system in a strange city, or read a compass in a forest. When Kate was quite young, I (Brad) asked her to take us to our luggage after landing in the airport. To do this, she had to follow the signs to baggage claim, which might seem easy to an adult, but for someone who's young and shy, it was difficult. When Kate made a correct turn, Mary and I would say, "Way to go!" or we'd give her a high-five. If she made a wrong turn, I'd make a goofy face and then she'd laugh and go back to look for the baggage claim sign. The point is, make it fun!

One child we know suggested finding her way home from a friend's house that was 15 minutes away. She chose the route by instinct, making a few wrong turns but knowing enough to backtrack and eventually got them home. Her father reported that his daughter was very pleased with figuring it out and he was also quite proud of her. She proved she could be a little more independent. Her reaction was "I had fun giving my dad directions. He was cool when I got lost."

If your child can't find the way, you could give hints: "Look at the street numbers. Do they tell you anything?" You may want to just stop the game if you sense that your child is getting so frustrated that nothing will help her find the way, even your hints. It's important not to make her feel that she failed a test, though. To avoid this reaction, say something like "Hey, you almost got us there. You made 10 correct turns and only one wrong turn. You tried to figure it out and that's the important thing. If we had more time, you could get that last turn, too, but why don't we just stop the game now so we'll be sure to get to the movie before it starts." Or, if it's true, you could say, "I'm not very good at directions either. It was hard for me to learn, too. That's why I'm giving you practice while I'm here to help, so you won't get lost as much as I do when you grow up."

When children are comfortable reading, you can also use Navigator as a way to teach them about maps. A word of warning: concepts that seem simple and obvious to adults may not even exist in a child's mind. I (Kate) remember a Sunday afternoon hike when I was the navigator and using a map. I must have made a wrong turn because my father asked in a surprised voice, "Kate, which way is north?" I pointed straight ahead: on maps at school, north was always at the top.

I (Brad) remember being very surprised by that conversation, realizing that I needed to do more to show Kate how to orient herself. I asked Kate where the sun set and which direction that was. Then, I turned the map so Kate and the map were facing the same way and asked her to point to west on the map and on the trail. Don't expect your child to master the points of a compass and orient herself to a map during one game of Navigator: this is a skill that takes instruction and practice. If it seems simple and easy to you, think of all the arguments you've witnessed between a driver and the map-reading adult passenger!

You can keep this challenge interesting for your child not only by using different destinations but also by alternating the way you orient yourself to a map, whether it's by the sun, local landmarks, street numbers and names, or compass. Kids who are five years and older can be shown a globe and taught how a compass points north, but younger kids may not grasp this concept.

Navigator is almost always popular with teenagers who are keen on getting their driver's license. They want to be able to use the car and get places on their own; you can use this desire to help them learn about maps and directions. Teenagers who consider themselves far too grown-up for other kinds of pretend games may be delighted to play Navigator.

Plan a Trip

When your children are responsible enough and resourceful enough to go on a trip by themselves, your role as a parent is very different. Instead of guiding and encouraging them, your job is to be there as a resource. Whether they're going on a day trip or a weekend away without parents, it's important to let them plan it. Ask questions to be sure they cover important details concerning safety, budget, and time schedules. Parents can and should set parameters or guidelines and insist that their kids follow them, but leave it up to the kids to figure out *how* to follow them. The following story from a friend, Trina, shows a good balance between sensible parental precautions and overprotection.

> Senior year in high school there were about eight of us, four girls and four guys, who were really good friends. One Monday, when all had off from school, one of the guys said, "Wouldn't it be fun to get away for the whole weekend?"
>
> I said, "Let's! I'll look into it."
>
> I found a place about seven hours' away and asked my parents if we could all go. They had a few questions:
>
> "Who's going?" (They knew and liked all the kids—a good start.)
>
> "Do all the parents know that their kids are going to be there?"
>
> "Who will be driving? What are their driving records?"
>
> "Will there be any couples there?" (Couples, they felt, would be putting too much temptation in our way. It was one thing to let couples spend the night at our house after a party, because everyone knew my parents could walk in at any minute; it was quite another when we were staying at a hotel.)
>
> "How much is it going to cost?"
>
> I hadn't thought about that part. I called a few places to get room rates. A friend was in charge of maps and actually getting us there, and another friend figured out how much gas that would take, while I drove. My dad asked, "How do you know this was the best motel price?"
>
> I said, "Because I called four different places ...."
>
> "You comparison shopped! Good for you, Trina!"
>
> My parents' last request was "Call when you get there, call every day just to check in—not for long, just to say 'hi, everything's fine, love you, bye.'"
>
> That was it. They could have asked more questions—but they left the rest of it—the details—up to us.

When your parents do that, you want to be worthy of that trust. We *all* felt that way; it was something that everyone understood. ... I told my friends, "This is under my name, or my family's name—if there is damage to the walls or the chandelier, I'm going to get in trouble and you're going to have to pay for it." As it turned out, the leg of a chair did get broken—and the guy who did it paid me for it and I paid my parents. After the weekend was over, my parents asked questions, but only of the most general kind: "How did it go? What was the best part? What was the worst? Is there anything you would have done differently?"

I thought back over the weekend. It was the first time my friends and I had ever shopped for and planned a meal together. We wanted to make a homemade spaghetti dinner and we did. But the shopping and cooking took so much time that I wished we had just brought something with us— then we would have had more time on the ski slope. That was the *only* thing I would have done differently.

This weekend was an almost perfect test of the kids' readiness for doing things alone, unchaperoned, and unsupervised. Trina and her friends were ready for the responsibility of planning a weekend trip and behaving within their parents' guidelines. The parameters Trina's parents set were just right, too, and her parents followed them as well. When Trina called, her parents kept the conversation brief: they just asked if she was having a good time and left it at that. We think that it's perfectly reasonable for parents to ask for a contact number (someone's cell phone, hotel information, a way that they can reach their child if necessary), but *not* to call every hour on the hour to find out what's going on. Calling every hour defeats the whole purpose of this activity, sending mixed messages about trust. When you *do* really trust your children with this kind of freedom, it's because you have prepared them to handle that freedom in a responsible way. As Trina said, "When parents can trust you, you can trust yourself. It's a building block; you want to be trustworthy so you can keep that trust—you want to be trustworthy *and* you want to be responsible. We all were both because we wanted more trips like that!"

Trust is the culmination of smaller amounts of trust and responsibility. Good parents give their kids as much freedom as they can handle and send the message that they *trust* their children to handle it. Parents who shelter and overprotect their children are sending a very different message: "You're not competent, you're not capable, so we're going to be right here, taking care of you." When these children go out into the world, they're unprepared for it; they don't know how to handle the choices and freedom.

I (Kate) remember, when I first got to college, being able to spot the can-do kids and distinguish them from the others. It was obvious: the can-do kids had fun, stayed safe, and got their work done. The kids who hadn't been given freedom and responsibility were the ones who drank too much, made fools of themselves, and put themselves in danger. To prepare your children for the coming college years, let them find their own path away from you when they're ready to travel.

Note

1. Richard Branson, *Sir Richard Branson: The Autobiography*. London: The Longman Publishing Group, 2002.

CHAPTER 11

UNDERSTAND HOW OTHERS SEE YOU

"Hey," Stradlater said. "Wanna do me a big favor?"

"What?" I said. Not too enthusiastic. He was always asking you to do him a big favor. You take a very handsome guy, or a guy that thinks he's a real hot-shot, and they're always asking you to do them a big favor. Just because they're crazy about themselves, they think you're crazy about them, too, and that you're just dying to do them a favor. It's sort of funny, in a way.

—*J.D. Salinger,* The Catcher in the Rye[1]

HEN KIDS UNDERSTAND HOW others see them, they have an advantage, both in getting along with other people and in assessing situations realistically. This type of self-perception grounds them in reality, so they don't go to the extremes of "Everyone hates me" or, equally destructive, "Everyone adores me; I can do no wrong." Seeing themselves realistically can also be a catalyst for change. Realizing how much other people like them can help shy children develop social skills and self-assurance; similarly, understanding how their bragging looks to others can help self-styled hot-shots like Stradlater tone themselves down.

> When people, either children or adults, know their strengths, they're more likely to participate and possibly shine in a particular area.

And when people, either children or adults, know their strengths, they're more likely to participate and possibly shine in a particular area, just as knowing their shortcomings helps them to prepare for potential challenges. It's hard to be a can-do kid with inaccurate, unrealistic assumptions about how people perceive and react to you. In this chapter, we give you three ways to help your children see themselves as they really are:

- Play a game that encourages them to imagine what their friends think of them.

- Videotape your children at social or family gatherings, then play back the tape and discuss the behavior. This exercise almost forces children to see themselves realistically.

- Intervene after a crisis or an argument with a friend. Your questions and the ensuing discussion may help your child see his or her own behavior with open eyes.

What works for one child may not work for another; that's why there are three choices for this activity. Younger children, for example, may enjoy the game option more than older children, but this isn't a hard-and-fast rule. The game can be varied for older children; some may find it fascinating as well as fun.

Pretend to Be Your Friends

Ask your child to think of three to five friends and imagine what each of those friends thinks about him or her. "What does this friend like most about you?" and "What does the friend like least about you?"

Time: 10 to about 30 minutes.

Venue: Any place you can talk and one of you can write.

Equipment: Something to write with.

Write down your child's answers, then read each back and ask your child what he or she thinks of that description. Write that down too. You can do this matter-of-factly or you can make it more fun by setting it up as a celebrity interview, as one father did with his daughter, Joan.

> "Pretend that you are Patty," he said, handing his daughter Joan a pretend microphone. "Patty, from your point of view—and take as long as you need to think about this—why do you like Joan?" (Use the pretend microphone only if your child is young enough to find such things fun!)
>
> "I like Joan because Joan's nice."
>
> "In what ways? Tell me more about how she's nice."
>
> Then, when he had a detailed enough answer, he asked, "What bothers you about Joan? Can you give me an example?"
>
> "I don't like it that Joan is always with Marsha on the playground. She should play more with me."

When your child has answered for all of her friends and you've written down all of the descriptions, you transition into a discussion. You can say something like "OK, now you're back to being Joan. Do you agree with how Patty would describe you? Are you nice and should you play with her more on the playground? Or do you disagree? If so, why?"

Your child's assessment is an important part of this process. Talk about it until she's expressed her thoughts. You may need to draw answers out of her. This is an activity that some children will find fascinating, some will find baffling, and others will find threatening. It's not easy for most of us to say how others would criticize us. But don't worry; there are other ways to help your child look at the world through other people's eyes.

> It's not easy for most of us to say how others would criticize us.

See Yourself on Video

The Smart family once visited family friends at their ranch. It was a really fun weekend, filled with animals and kids and all kinds of outdoor activities, which the parents avidly filmed with a new video camera. At one point, Kate's brother got on the pony bareback. Both families watched as it ran around the yard, with Geoff bouncing up and down on its back. Kate thought Geoff looked really silly: he couldn't really control the pony. Proud of her own riding and eager to impress her parents' friends, she said, "Geoff, you don't know how to ride! I can do much better!" I (Brad) scolded, "Kate, what a terrible thing to say! You know your brother doesn't ride and he's giving it his best."

See Yourself on Video

Time: You may need to do this several times to find a scene that shows your child's social behavior.

Venue: A social or family occasion for the first part, anyplace you can play a video for the second part.

Equipment: A video camera, a video player.

I (Kate) recall being really annoyed at the time, even angry, at my dad for embarrassing me in front of everyone. After all, what I'd said was true. Geoff couldn't ride; I could. What was the big deal? Then I forgot about it—until we got home and were excitedly watching the video and reminiscing about the fun weekend. We got to that part where I made fun of Geoff and I was shocked at what I saw. I felt awful. It was such a mean thing to say. I could tell by the expressions on everyone else's faces in the video that they thought so too. Those looks were far more powerful than words. I realized that I'd been bragging to the group, trying to impress everyone at Geoff's expense, and I just looked bratty and *mean*.

For the video technique to work, you need to do it often enough or unobtrusively enough to capture your kids' typical social or family behavior rather than their acting for the camera. Do it at large family gatherings or social occasions during an activity or video your kids so routinely that they forget that the camera is there. That way, when you watch the video together with your children, they see their behavior realistically. Don't just look for problem behavior. Try to capture positives on tape, and then use praise. For example, if a small child tripped and your son showed sympathy and helped the child, you might say, "That was very nice of you to help."

Intervene: Use a Crisis to Discover Empathy

Sometimes children who aren't normally given to self-analysis or reflection are willing to look at their own behavior during a social crisis—when they've just had a fight with a friend, or someone is being mean to them, or they're just not getting along with their peers and don't understand why.

This is a great time to use the SMART Decision Pad. You can say something like, "I understand that you're going through a difficult time with _____. Do you want to talk about it?" or "One of the things that helped me when I was your age was to take a step back and see the situation in a different way. Would you be willing to do this? Would you like to try it? You can involve me as much as you want or you can do this on your own."

Then just play it by ear, remembering to listen a lot and ask questions when appropriate: "What happened in the fight? What's your take on it? How do you feel about it?" It's hard to know where someone else is coming from when you're wrapped up in your own emotions. So listen to your child until she has expressed her feelings—and *then* ask her to think about her friend's feelings with questions like "What did your friend say? How do you think she feels about it then and right now?"

For most children, middle school is full of crises that will give parents plenty of chances to try this activity, though at some point many children (especially those who have been raised to be resourceful) will take pride in being able to sort out these situations for themselves and figure out what their friends are feeling without involving you at all. Then help your child use the SMART Decision Pad to figure out what to do. Self-awareness is most valuable when converted to positive action. A child who concludes he has peer problems

> Self-awareness is most valuable when converted to positive action.

because he won't do drugs might pick an option: get new friends.

Our friend Chantelle remembers befriending a new girl at school in ninth grade, thinking she was doing a really nice thing. Then she found a note in her locker from her best friend, Thomasine, saying she wasn't a good friend at all, in fact she was "a disloyal bitch." Chantelle had no idea what Thomasine was talking about, and her first reaction was to get mad. Then when she calmed down, she thought to herself, "Why would Thomasine be angry with me? If I were in her shoes, why would *I* be mad at my best friend?" Chantelle didn't know—it was puzzling and hurtful. It became a mystery to solve: she went over the clues and evidence in her mind following the SMART Decision Pad. That helped her realize her goal was not to get back at Thomasine, but to become friends again.

First, she needed to understand why Thomasine was mad at her. "OK, where have I seen her? What classes do we have together? What did I say to her at lunch? Oh, I didn't see her at lunch, I sat with Callie." At that moment, she realized that Thomasine was probably feeling left out because of her new friendship with Callie. So Chantelle called Thomasine and asked, "Are you mad at me because I've been spending a lot of time with Callie lately?" Thomasine said, "Yes! Do you not like me anymore because I have braces?" Callie was a slim, beautiful blond with perfect skin, so Chantelle started to see how left out and insecure Thomasine felt. They ended up having a good conversation that saved their friendship, which was Chantelle's original goal. Both girls learned that they could stay best friends and still spend time with other people—Chantelle's other goal.

People who can analyze situations, gain self-awareness, and act the way Chantelle did have an enormous advantage, not only in getting along with others, but generally in life. You can give your children that advantage by repeating or coming up with variations on this activity until they routinely understand how others see them.

Note

1. J.D. Salinger, *The Catcher in the Rye.* New York: Bantam Books, 1972.

CHAPTER 12

INTRODUCE YOURSELF AND START A CONVERSATION

Mary Power and Laura looked into the mirror, and with their fingers fluffed up their bangs, slightly flattened by their hoods. Then in the friendliest way Mrs. Woodworth said, "If you've finished your primping, come into the sitting room."

Ida and Minnie, Arthur and Cap and Ben were already there. Mrs. Woodworth said, "Now when Jim comes home from work, our party will be complete." She sat down and began to talk pleasantly. After a few moments Mrs. Woodworth excused herself and went into the kitchen. Then a stillness settled on everyone. Laura felt she should say something, but she could think of nothing to say. Her feet seemed too big and she did not know what to do with her hands.

She looked at the other girls, and knew that she must say something, for no one else could. Yet it was more than she could do, to break that silence. Her heart sank.

—*Laura Ingalls Wilder,* Little Town on the Prairie[1]

F YOU CAN REMEMBER FEELING that young and awkward—completely unable to talk when you met someone, even when you knew you should—you know why your children need to learn to say hello and begin a conversation. Being able to do this easily gives your children poise and social skills that they'll be able to count on for the rest of their lives.

Parents who take the time to teach their children how to meet and greet people are doing everyone a favor, not just their children. Think how you feel when you go to someone's house and the children just go right on with what they're doing, ignoring you completely. We feel hurt when that happens—and insulted too. We also think less of the parents for not having taught their children better manners and an important life skill. Consider how you feel when the children greet you or introduce themselves as though they're glad to see you. That's what this activity teaches your children to do. This is what you do:

- Talk to your child about why it's important to be able to greet people gracefully and politely.
- Role-play an introduction with your child. Then comment on it.
- Watch your child introduce himself or herself in a real situation. Afterwards, comment on it.

Introduce Yourself and Start a Conversation

Time: About 20 minutes the first time, 10 minutes for each practice session. This is an activity you will probably repeat often; the main benefits come from repeating the practice until the behavior becomes second nature.

Venue (practice): At home, in a car, any place private where you can both talk.

Venue (real): Any place your child would meet someone.

Equipment: None.

The commentary is important: many benefits come from this feedback and from repeated practice. If you do this over and over, it becomes so natural that children introduce themselves and begin conversations without even having to think about it, even in situations that might once have made them shy or uncomfortable.

Explain the Purpose

Begin by talking with your children about why it's important to learn how to introduce themselves to people. If they're shy, you can tell them that this activity will help them meet people, make friends, become more comfortable socially, and make social occasions more fun for them and for the people they're meeting. Older children may also be reminded that first impressions really do count. Psychologists have found that most people make up their minds about others within 30 seconds of meeting them, and even something as simple as how you shake hands and introduce yourself creates a big—and sometimes lasting—impression.

When people greet us warmly and seem genuinely interested in us, it's not just polite; it begins a relationship. It invites us to reciprocate, to show interest in the other person. *Every* successful businessperson learns the social niceties. In contrast, when we meet people who avoid eye contact and seem to be merely going through the motions as they say hello, we naturally conclude that they are not interested in us and feel little desire to continue the conversation, let alone start a relationship. We all remember handshakes that felt like cold fish, others that were so firm that they felt like the first move in a wrestling match, and others that were just right—both friendly and firm. A very successful associate remembers that as a child (and even as an adult) people sometimes looked surprised when they met her and said, "Great handshake!" That always pleased her and her parents.

> When people greet us warmly and seem genuinely interested in us, it's not just polite; it begins a relationship.

You can start giving your children these experiences when they are very young. Even children as young as three and four can learn to say hello, introduce themselves, and shake hands. You don't need to go into all of the reasons; a simple "It's what polite people do" should be explanation enough. When adults respond politely and warmly to their greetings, young children learn for themselves that introductions make meeting new people more pleasant.

One sidenote: different cultures have particular customs when it comes to greetings and introductions. In some cultures, for example, looking an older person in the eye is rude and shaking hands is an unthinkable familiarity. We're not saying that the examples we use here represent the global standard. The important thing is for your child to know how to introduce himself or herself confidently and comfortably, and to do it in such a way that the other person feels comfortable and respected, too. That's the goal; the actual words and the handshake we use are just one way of getting there.

Role-Play the Greeting, Comment

Role-playing is most effective when it's followed by a real meeting with a friendly adult. When such a person comes over, suggest that your child go to the door, let the person in, and introduce himself or herself. Some parents tell the child something interesting about the adult ("She just got back from Africa" or "She was a bridesmaid at our wedding") or show the child a photograph of the visitor prior to her arrival. Then, just say, "Let's practice."

For us, this meant that Brad would explain what Kate was expected to do: smile and look the person in the eye, call him or her by name ("Hello Mr. Jones.") introduce herself ("I'm Kate."), and firmly shake hands. When she was a little older, practice included initiating a conversation. But at first, just a good greeting was enough.

We think it's important to actually practice this, even though it sounds so simple and obvious, because when something is new for kids, they can get nervous.

We think it's important to actually practice this, even though it sounds so simple and obvious, because when something is new for kids, they can get nervous—and when they get nervous, they can forget. Practice also gives you the parent a chance to make comments. For example, when you're showing your child how to shake hands, you can say things like "A little bit firmer, not that hard, that's just right."

When the child has learned the greeting —smile, look the person in the eye, greet him or her by name, introduce self, shake hands—you can reinforce it with a little dress rehearsal. I (Brad) would actually go outside, ring the doorbell (most children find this kind of play-acting fun), and wait for Kate to let me in.

When Kate was comfortable greeting people and had done it successfully with many adults, she was taught to initiate some kind of conversation. There are several ways you can do this, such as:

- Tell the child a little bit about the person before he or she arrives and let the child come up with conversation starters.
- Prepare a couple of throw-out questions in advance. For example, you could suggest, "How was the traffic?" or if the dog barks, "Fido doesn't bite."

When children are first moving on to initiating a conversation with an adult, the goal is for them to say something that stimulates a response. You can help by giving them ideas. Don't worry if it's obvious to the adult that the child was scripted. That's OK! Adults are delighted to go along with the program and your child learns how to engage people—and adults at that. When your children become comfortable introducing themselves (which may take several months), they can think of their own conversation starters. But in the beginning it's perfectly fine to suggest something like "Mr. Jones is a history teacher and so you could say, 'I understand you're a history teacher. What's your favorite period in American history?' or 'I wrote a paper on the Civil War last year and I loved it.'" Whatever you decide they're ready to do, role-play the greeting and make specific comments afterwards: "I felt so welcome when you smiled and said my name—and that was a great handshake."

Do It for Real, Analyze It Afterwards

After role-playing, do it for real and discuss how it went later after the guests have gone. Even when our neighbors, Sophie and her father, Ben, had practiced and Sophie had done it perfectly with her father, she'd sometimes clam up when she met a "real adult." Her father would usually be within hearing distance while the greetings were going on, and he was very consistent about making comments later: "Great handshake, very polite, you seemed poised—but I notice you didn't call him by name." Then they would practice a couple of times and he'd praise her. As always, praising the four steps done well makes it easy for the child to improve on the fifth step.

Sophie recalls, "It was good because my dad kept working with me. I'd greet someone, he'd nicely suggest any improvement and eventually I got it right. It became second nature." That's the goal: to get to the point where your child is not trying, doesn't feel tested, and it just becomes what they do when meeting someone.

If your child is very self-conscious or feels awkward or silly as you practice, encourage her to practice anyway: "It's OK and understandable to feel silly, but you'll like it and feel proud of yourself when you do it tonight. Come on, one more time. I'm Mr. Jones. I'll step outside to the door and ring the doorbell, and you greet me." Even though it was hard for Sophie to do it at first, it was nice when her parents said things like "Ms. Smith told us how polite and interested you were in her."

Learning to greet people and start a conversation is rewarding for the child: Sophie blossomed from shy and quiet to self-assured and engaging.

I (Kate) and my husband, Chris, recently flew to Arizona to visit my cousin Ann and her family. (Months earlier, Ann read a draft of this book and said she would do the greeting activity with her six-year-old son, Jack.) Before we were even out of the car, Jack came running over. His friend came running up behind him, both holding little squirt guns. "Hi, Kate!" Jack said, giving me a big hug. He greeted Chris by name, too, and shook his hand. Then he said, "This is my friend José. We met when we lived in Mexico. He is visiting for the weekend, just like you." Jack's greeting was charming and natural and it made us feel so welcome. That night at dinner we both told my cousin how impressed we had been by her son's greeting. Ann and her husband looked so happy and proud!

Note

1. Laura Ingalls Wilder, *Little Town on the Prairie*. New York: Harper and Row, 1985.

LEARN ACTIVE LISTENING

Listen, or your tongue will make you deaf.

—Native American Proverb

E INTRODUCED THE CONCEPT OF ACTIVE listening earlier in the book. In this chapter, we'll drill down into the tactics that allow you to engage in active listening with your child. Active listening is repeating back or paraphrasing what people have said, to show that you understand their words and their feelings. Active listening shows understanding and respect, and empathy; it doesn't impose judgments.

It sounds something like this: "So you're saying that you ...." (not "You should have ...."). When it's appropriate, active listeners show empathy: "That must be very frustrating."

When you listen actively, you show that you're paying attention to what is being communicated—both to the actual words and to their emotional content. If, for example, someone says, "My purse got stolen!" an active listener would say something like, "That must have been terrifying! Are you OK?" Responses such as "Did you report it? Oh, you should call the police right away!" or "Where were you? What were you doing in that neighborhood, anyway?" are also appropriate, but do not convey the deeper understanding and empathy of active listening.

Active listening is something many people go through life without ever learning, leading to a lifetime of difficulty communicating with others. It's not easy being around a person who listens with dead, empty eyes or who interrupts to say, "Oh, that happened to me once!" and proceeds to tell his or her own story.

I (Brad) have coached thousands of high achievers; my most common recommendation to them has been "You are successful, but you can be even more successful if you learn and use active listening." In hundreds of thousands of surveys I've done, I've found that most people who report to high achievers want those bosses to become better listeners. People who are good listeners are usually praised for being understanding, respectful, empathetic, open-minded, good at preventing conflicts, appreciative, and persuasive. Wow, that's a lot of strengths! And that's why the best leaders are active listeners.

> People who are good listeners are usually praised for being understanding, respectful, empathetic, open-minded, good at preventing conflicts, appreciative, and persuasive. Wow!

Listening well builds relationships. One important technique in marital counseling is to help spouses *both* actively listen. Communication is much more effective when everyone actively listens. People who really know how to listen show this ability with their words, eyes, and body language. And they ask follow-up questions. Active listening involves paying attention to the person who's speaking and showing that you are paying attention in every way you can.

One of the best ways to teach your children to actively listen is to do it yourself, to model it consistently and carefully. But you don't *always* have to be a terrific listener. Indeed, there are times when it is inappropriate to listen: "I'd love to listen to your story, but I have to pay attention to the traffic right now. Would you tell me when we get home?" Instead of pretending to listen (as many people do, especially on the telephone), it's much better to say, "I'm right in the middle of something right now. Can you call me back when I'm not so distracted?"

It can be instructive to talk about listening. For instance, when the family has been at any kind of gathering, talk afterwards about who listened well, who didn't, what it felt like when you were talking to someone who listened to you. You can be specific; before a gathering, tell your children that later you'll all talk about the best and worst listeners. Then you can compare people at the party: inevitably the most interesting, engaging people were the *active* listeners and the most boring people were the ones who talked about themselves and showed only perfunctory interest in others. In the business world, "consultative selling" is the basis for many sales training programs. Trainees learn, "If you want to impress people, *first* listen carefully to their needs, *then* show you understand, and *finally* explain how you can help them." Consultative selling relies on active listening.

Learn Active Listening

Time: 10 to 20 or 30 minutes and even longer.

Venue: Any place you can talk.

Equipment: Something to write with (optional).

The activities in this chapter give your children practice in active listening. There are three: one to teach the basics of facial expressions, one to show how listening is practiced, and one that's a little more complicated, involving nonverbal active listening or body language. Briefly they look like this:

- **Game 1:** You draw a face and your child tells you what the person is feeling.

- **Game 2:** Your child tells a story and you listen actively—paraphrasing, empathizing, and clarifying. You repeat the story as accurately as you can. Then, at the end, ask your child how you did as a listener and talk about it. Then, *if* your child wants to, you switch roles.

- **Game 3:** Your child talks and you use body language—*only* body language—to show that you're listening. As you do this, notice how your child responds. At the end, talk about how you each acted and felt during the conversation. Then have your child talk again. This time, let your body language show that you're *not* paying any attention at all. Talk about that afterwards, too. You may both be surprised at how dramatically different the two conversations are!

The techniques this chapter teaches can help you too. Active listening works in all relationships, including those with your children. Several years ago I (Brad) taught a course in active listening at Northwestern University. Several parents volunteered that they hadn't had meaningful conversations with their children in a long time. Within two weeks, after only two classes, most parents reported that they were finally connecting with their kids. As one mother said, "I realized that almost all of my communication with my daughter had been critical, nosey, and negative. With active listening I was *not* judgmental—I just showed interest in what she was experiencing and communicating. And she responded."

Identify Facial Expressions

Active listeners are empathetic and one way to help a young child learn to become more empathetic is to help her identify facial expressions. You can draw a face and ask the child what the person is feeling or which face is happiest, saddest, etc. When your child gets good at attaching the correct feeling to a face, you can ask him or her to draw the faces while you identify the feelings. Or you can make a face and ask your child to name your expression.

| Grumpy | Sad | Happy |
| Embarrassed | Excited | Angry |

Tell and Repeat Stories

This is a game that teaches some basics of active listening: paying attention to what the other person is saying and showing that you understand it. The basic game is simple, and the advanced form is not.

The basic game is telling a story and the other person repeats it. Next time your child complains, "Mom, you're not listening to me!" say, "I'm sorry—there are some Smart Parenting activities on listening. Maybe we should try one so I can improve."

You go first. Tell a story to your child—a one-minute, straightforward story for an eight-year-old, and a more complex and longer story for older children. Your child repeats it, and you say if your child listened well, or not so well. Then switch roles. Make it fun—if your child didn't repeat the part where you accidentally dropped the hamburgers in the fire, have a laugh about it. You'll both conclude that constant listening isn't so easy.

When you and your child think you are ready for the advanced version, read the rules:

- One of you recites a five-minute story.
- The other looks for five to ten opportunities to interject brief active listening comments such as:

  "So you're saying…"

  "You felt…"

Active listening interjections are intended to clarify what happened, empathize with the story teller, and *prove* listening was very good.

Anyone can learn active listening interjections, but it takes practice. Parents will be doing well to "pull off" three or four active listening comments. When your child says, "The fire alarm bell went off next to my head and I jumped," an example of an active listening interjection might be, "That must have scared the willies out of you!" and your child might reply, "You know it! I almost peed in my pants!" A less sensitive reply might be, "Why would a builder put the alarm bell inside a classroom?" Your child doesn't want your architectural commentary, but instead would appreciate your understanding what it was like for her to experience the crisis.

If your child wants to try the advanced version, praise the effort. If she makes ten attempts and one or two were successful, be thankful. If some attempts seemed forced or inaccurate (she mis-heard you), discuss it in a light, positive way: "I said there were four people, not three, but good for you for repeating all the other points!"

An advantage of this activity is that after doing it a couple of times, both parents and children report they become better at active listening. They both recognize when the other is listening better, they "spot" the active listening interjections, and they apply those skills more and more when they are listening to parents, friends, and teachers.

Show You're Listening with Body Language

One dramatic way to teach your child about body language is to make a game out of it. In this game, one person talks and the other person uses body language—only body language—to indicate how interested he or she is. This teaches the nonverbal part of active listening.

You can repeat this several times, once with the listener's body language saying, "Yes, I'm interested, I'm really listening!" and again with it saying, "No, I'm not interested, I'm not paying attention to you at all, and I wish you'd be quiet!" Begin by talking about—or, better yet, demonstrating—the difference between the two attitudes. You can act out the body language, asking your child what it "says" or you can flip through a magazine, looking for photographs of people talking, and ask your child about them: "Is that person listening? Not listening? How can you tell?" Figure 13-1 shows some contrasting examples.

This game will probably work best if you are the listener the first few times: it's harder to be the listener than the talker, and most of the responsibility in this game is the listener's! Begin by asking a question about something you know your child wants to tell you about: that should get things off to a lively start. Then pay attention as hard as you can by looking your child in the eye, leaning forward, and saying, "Mm-hmm" when appropriate. Let your face mirror your child's. Above all, don't interrupt and don't make judgments. Your children are probably very good at reading your expressions—just how good might surprise

Listening	Not Listening
Look at the speaker	Look around, or at something else
Lean toward the speaker	Turn away from the speaker
Nod and shake your head appropriately, or mirror the speaker's facial expressions	Remain impassive, or yawn
Let your body mirror the other person's body	Cross your arms, swing your leg, fiddle with your hair or your fingers or clothes
Smile encouragingly (or whatever expression would be appropriate)	Laugh during serious comments, sigh when the other person says something funny (in other words: respond inappropriately to what was just said)

Figure 13-1. Body language: listening and not listening you.

Immediately after the story is told, write down or notice how your child responded to your listening and attentiveness. When someone is actively listening, most talkers open up, speaking more, becoming more animated, smiling more, and sitting or standing in a more relaxed way. Their eyes light up, they seem more energetic, and they may even seem more alive.

Then you *both* talk about your reactions—what you each noticed about the other's reactions, how you each felt during the conversation. Switch roles: you tell a story and your child uses the positive body language. Then he writes down his reactions and the two of you discuss them. Next, do the entire activity again with a different topic and the opposite body language: look away, fidget, frown, turn away. How does your child respond to that? Does she stop smiling, shorten her story, talk louder, or tug at your sleeve?

The difference between the two conversations will probably be dramatic—and the listener's emotional reactions to the conversation may be as profoundly different as the speaker's. Our guess is that you'll both find the conversation awkward when the listener isn't paying attention. The speaker may find it hard to tell the story and you may both get somewhat irritable. In fact, the not-listening conversation may be so awkward that you'll both want to keep it pretty short; few people are self-confident or thick-skinned enough to keep talking when the person they're addressing is obviously bored and impatient.

If your children enjoy this game, encourage them to play it with friends. They may learn things about themselves and each other that they wouldn't learn with you. When a person's body language shows that he or she is listening, both people usually become more interested in the conversation.

We encourage you to learn and practice active listening, not only to model it for your children, but to help you bond with them. Active listening isn't just a simple technique; it is an act that enables human connection. The beauty of it is that most people can learn it, understand it, and actually perform it well with practice. But even people who aren't naturally sensitive, perceptive, or interested in others can learn this skill. And in the process, they develop more satisfying relationships with people.

> When a person's body language shows that he or she is listening, both people usually become more interested in the conversation.

CHAPTER 14

FIND WAYS TO MAKE FRIENDS

The making of friends, who are real friends, is the best token of success in life.

—*Edward Everett Hale*

You don't want to go making friends with the wrong sort.

—*Harry Potter in*
Harry Potter and the Sorcerer's Stone

MOST FRIENDSHIPS GROW GRADUALLY out of common activities, interests, and values. For some people, friendships seem to begin and grow easily and naturally—almost effortlessly—all their lives. Sometimes though, if a family moves, or a child changes schools, or just grows older and develops different interests, making friends can become difficult. And of course, some children are just shy.

If your child doesn't have many friends at the moment, this chapter will show you how to use the SMART Decision Pad to help figure out ways to make new ones. That's all the part you'll play—the actual friend-making is up to your child. Your job is to encourage the decision-making process by choosing a good time to have the discussion(s) and then just be a facilitator. In this chapter you will do the following:

- Gradually introduce the topic in a way that will build your child's self-assurance.
- Use the SMART Decision Pad (concentrating on the brainstorming step) and active listening to help your child figure out ways to make friends.

Find Ways to Make Friends

Time: Wait for the right moment to have this discussion; the discussion(s) could take from 10 minutes to half an hour.

Venue: Any place you and your child can talk.

Equipment: None needed.

Bring up the Subject

Not having friends can be painful to discuss. If your child is very sensitive about it or you're not sure he or she will welcome your help, wait for him or her to bring it up.

> Not having friends can be painful to discuss.

You could approach the subject indirectly with a general discussion about what makes a good friend and what doesn't, paying particular attention to qualities your child has and giving your child plenty of praise for having those qualities. If, for example, your child says that a good friend is loyal, reminisce about specific times when he showed loyalty. Such praise encourages children, makes them confident that they have something to offer, and helps them draw on the qualities in themselves that they can use to make friends or, as you may want to phrase it, "get to know people better." This conversation may help your child come out and say that he wishes he had more friends. If your child seems too uncomfortable, back away from the topic. Try again another day.

Figure Out How to Do It

When your child shows interest in making friends, there are several ways to approach figuring out what to do about it. You can ask if your child would like to use the SMART Decision Pad to think of ways to meet more people or get to know people better. For example, you can ask the question, "What are some places here in (wherever you live) that you could meet people or get to know someone better?" When your child answers, encourage him or her to give you even more answers. Brainstorm ideas until one comes up that your child is really enthusiastic about. If your child doesn't say anything, you can suggest one or two, as examples to show what you mean. Then ask again: "Talking to someone on the bus might be one place. Where else? What are some other places you can do that?" If your child gravitates toward making friends with kids you approve of, great! If not, the SMART Decision Pad can clarify the advantages of having certain friends and the disadvantages of befriending others (as Harry Potter noticed).

You can go through the whole decision-making model with your child: brainstorm to help think of ideas, ask questions, and listen to help him or her pick the best option if that's necessary. It may not be, because one choice may be obviously appealing and doable. Then figure out a plan for implementing it. How much you push your child in this conversation depends on the situation and on your child; some children may actually welcome prodding while others may be put off by it. Or you could give your child a book. *How Kids Make Friends* by Lonnie Michelle is the kids' counterpart to Dale Carnegie's *How to Win Friends and Influence People*. It's lively, engaging, and even funny; as one young reviewer wrote, "By the time I finished reading it, my face hurt from smiling so much."

Another way to present this is to put your child in a "take charge" mode: "How nice would it be for Jenna if you included her in your day?" That way, your child feels that she's doing something for someone else, giving something to someone else. She isn't the needy one; she's the one who has friendship to give! Many children hesitate to admit they need, or have difficulty making, friends.

That's what one friend of ours did with her son, Holden. Holden had a small group of close friends, but he was also a little shy. There was one boy in their neighborhood, Hlee, who didn't have any friends. Hlee's family had just moved here from Laos. So our friend encouraged Holden to make friends with Hlee. Holden was afraid the other boys in his group would make fun of him if he did because Hlee was "different." Though Holden agreed with his mother that befriending Hlee would be a nice thing to do and he said he would do so, he balked. Holden's mother reminded him of his promise: "Why don't you have Hlee over? When are you going to have him visit?"

The key was finding a reason other than to "make friends." Hlee was good at math and, when Holden was struggling, our friend said, "Hlee can probably help you better than I can. Why don't you call him?"

So finally, Holden invited Hlee over and the boys became study mates. They'd each help the other with homework and have some fun, too. Holden learned that he could step outside the group without being ostracized by them—and he gained a new friend.

However you choose to approach the subject, remember that your kids are going to make mistakes as they put into practice the ideas you talk about. Let it happen. They'll learn fast; they don't need you to intervene and monitor this.

> Your kids are going to make mistakes as they put into practice the ideas you talk about. Let it happen.

When it comes to relationships with their peers, children are usually very sensitive—too sensitive, sometimes—and self-aware. They'll figure it out. As one client recalled:

I remember going over to Wendy's house. We were the same age, but she seemed very sophisticated to me. I tried hard—too hard—to impress her and make her like me.

The first time I went to her house—a huge mansion, with a tennis court, swimming pool, etc., I said, "Wow! How ostentatious!" thinking that "ostentatious" meant something like "impressive and beautiful." I thought I was being nice and showing off my sophisticated vocabulary. She gave me a weird look, but didn't say anything. It wasn't until I got home and looked up the word in the dictionary that I understood why. I couldn't believe I'd said something so tactless—how embarrassing!

I'd been trying to impress her with my great vocabulary; I should have just been sincere and said, "What a beautiful house!" At that moment, I realized that I should just be myself, and not try to act older, or more sophisticated—or put on any kind of act.

Once I started being myself, I relaxed and started to feel accepted at the new school; I knew the friendship was solid when Wendy invited me to her birthday party.

Friendships just kind of happen and then grow naturally. The best thing you can do for your children is give them some encouragement and help them think of places and situations where they might be likely to meet potential friends. Beyond that and welcoming friends to the house, it's best if you let your children figure out how to build friendships themselves.

> Friendships just kind of happen and then grow naturally. It's best if you let your children figure out how to build friendships themselves.

This may be an activity that works best when you leave the follow-through to your child and just back off. After you've prompted your child to construct and embrace a plan, don't badger her. Your knowledge of your child and your sensitivity will guide you. Sometimes, as in Holden's case, a little parental prodding was sufficient; without it nothing would have happened. But if his parents had nagged him to do more, he might have done nothing. Parents need to be sensitive; at times even asking how things are going can seem like a criticism or intrusion. At the stage of life when making friends becomes an issue, kids can be hypersensitive. One client remembers starting a new school and wanting to just figure out how to make friends on her own: "It was too uncomfortable to discuss with my parents at the time; I wasn't looking for a lecture on how to act appropriately."

As usual, your knowledge of your child is the best guide. If you sense that a question from you would be welcome, saying something like "Did you meet anyone interesting today?" can be a good way to show interest without implying anything negative. The question assumes that *your child* is the one calling the shots; he or she is the one deciding about the other people. If you use active listening when your child answers, you'll learn as much about how things are going as your child wants you to know—which, when it comes to making friends, is all you need to know.

Ultimately, the child is in control of making friends and building relationships. Parents can be there to encourage them and follow up with occasional questions to nudge them in a productive direction, like befriending kids with the right values. But parents can't make friends for their kids. If you show confidence in your children, they will acquire valuable relationship-building skills and more generally become a bit more resourceful, all the while making new friends.

CHAPTER 15

LEARN PUBLIC SPEAKING

Without question, most people think public speaking is more of an obstacle than an opportunity, more of a problem than a solution. But in fact, the exact reverse is true. There is no single greater opportunity for productivity, profit, and reward than the simple act of opening your mouth to tell your own story.

—*Granville N. Toogood,* The Articulate Executive[1]

WHEN A PERSON IS ARTICULATE, confident, poised, engaging, and interesting in a public forum, he or she will carry these qualities into every situation. Children who learn how to carry themselves in the same way will be more confident around other people, speaking up in class, leading peers, asserting themselves, and meeting people. Public speaking is part of the recipe for becoming a can-do kid! In this chapter, we give you two activities to teach your children how to become good public speakers:

- Make an extemporaneous speech.

- Videotape your child making a speech; then play it back and offer feedback.

■ Play a charades-like game in which everyone makes a speech.

Learn Public Speaking

Time: About half an hour to do the activity together; for the first activity, the child will prepare on his or her own. You will probably repeat the activity several times.

Venue: At home for the first activity, any place you can talk for the second activity.

Equipment: A video camera and player for the first activity; paper, pencil, and two other people (for a total of four) for the second activity.

Videotape Your Child

When I (Kate) had to make a presentation or give a speech as a child, I'd practice in front of my parents, who would give me feedback and suggestions. But even before rehearsing in front of them, I'd practice by myself until I was ready for my parents to videotape me. After they taped my presentation, I would watch the video with them and we'd critique it together.

This is a technique that is widely used among professionals, whether they are preparing for a media event, a job interview, or a public speech. And like many of them, I imagine, I remember how interesting and shocking it was to see myself on film, taking note of how many times I said "um" and "like," and to hear how nervous my voice sounded, which many times was a lot shakier than I really felt. I used this technique, over and over, until I perfected the presentation. And each time, there was always some improvement over my previous effort. The videotaping was much more effective than just practicing in front of the mirror or my parents alone. When I was satisfied after taping and critiquing myself, I asked my parents to be the "audience" and then to offer feedback.

The parental critique should include both praise as well as pointers on how to improve. It's important to heap praise on your child, not just when the speech is finally good, but whenever he or she makes *progress* of any kind. Be sincere and specific. Look for progress and respond by saying things like "Nice going! See how much more eye contact you're making?" or "Wow, you've stopped fidgeting with your hair!"

> It's important to heap praise on your child, not just when the speech is finally good, but whenever he or she makes *progress* of any kind.

In many schools, public speaking is a regular part of many classes. But it doesn't have to be something at school; you can manufacture occasions for speeches: a happy birthday wish, an after-dinner speech to welcome a visiting relative, or a toast at a holiday dinner. In our experience as professionals, we've found that with practice, most people can become good (not necessarily excellent) at public speaking. So if you agree it's a valuable skill, encouraging your child to find opportunities to speak might be necessary.

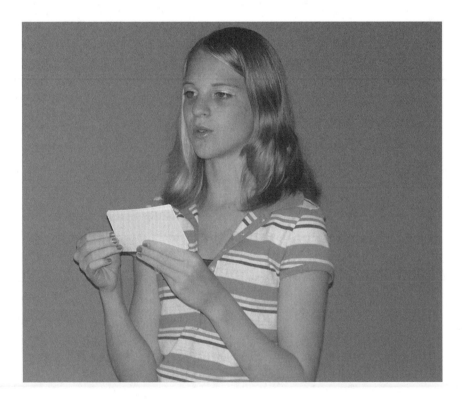

Make a Speech on the Fly

This activity is similar to charades. However, instead of acting something out physically, you make a speech. You need at least four people. This is a fun, instructive family activity, both for practiced speechmakers and for novices.

The game is simple. Each player gets a piece of paper and writes down a general topic (dogs, vacation spots, honesty, etc.); the only rule is that the topics have to be general. For example, "music" or even "rock" is allowed, but specific categories of music or particular songs are not. Everyone folds the paper the same way so no one can tell whose is whose and then puts the paper into a container, like a box or a hat. You shake them up and then have every player pick one. Each person takes a turn to make a speech; only the next speaker may open his or her paper. (This keeps the others from rehearsing their speech instead of listening to someone else's speech.) You can decide as a family what to do if a player picks his or her own topic from the container. We usually just went ahead and did it!

With the topic in hand, each person gives a three-minute speech consisting of an introduction, a body, and a concluding statement. There is one minute of preparation time to think of ideas and scribble down an outline or notes.

It's a fun activity because it's almost extemporaneous, and even experienced speechmakers can find themselves at a loss when confronted with a topic like "pencils" or "pink." It can be humorous too, when there's a disconnect between the speaker and the topic—when, say, an 11-year-old brother has to give a talk on pantyhose.

When kids learn to speak without much preparation in front of a group of people they also learn poise, presence of mind, and how to perform under pressure. Many times in life, when people have to say something or do something on the spot, they freeze up. This activity gives kids (and parents too)

> When kids learn to speak without much preparation in front of a group of people, they also learn poise, presence of mind, and how to perform under pressure.

practice at focusing, mobilizing their skills, and following through on the task at hand.

How often have you thought after a party or social event, "I wish I'd said ..."? The French even have a phrase for this—they call it "l'esprit de l'escalier" (staircase wit), from the days when people would leave large, formal parties by going down a long flight of stairs—and would only then think of witty remarks they wished they'd made. Maybe the activities in this chapter will help everyone in your family leave meetings pleased with what they did say rather than regretting what they didn't say.

These activities will help your children overcome the discomfort almost everyone feels when called upon to speak in public. It's normal for people to fear doing what they don't know how to do, especially when failure means being embarrassed in front of a group. Practice at public speaking helps your children overcome that fear, boosts their confidence, and gives them a life-long skill. When you take an active role in coaching your child to do even one good speech, he or she will be more likely to deliver a great speech with pride and welcome the next opportunity to speak in public.

Note

1. Granville N. Toogood, *The Articulate Executive*. New York: McGraw-Hill, 1997.

CHAPTER 16

BE A
TEAM PLAYER

The path to greatness is along with others.

    —*Baltasar Gracián,* Oráculo Manual y Arte de Prudencia[1]

All for one, one for all!

    —*Alexandre Dumas,* The Three Musketeers[2]

EVERYONE AGREES THAT BEING a good team player is essential in life and at work. It's just as important to know how to be a team member as to know how to be the leader—and to know which role is appropriate when. In this chapter, you give your child practice at all three skills by when you:

- Ask your children about their experiences on teams.
- Take your whole family to a ropes course center, where everyone will get to be both a team member and the leader.
- Talk about the experience afterwards.

Talk with Your Kids About Their Experiences on Teams

Begin this discussion by identifying those attributes and qualities that make a good team, not by listing attributes of good team members (that comes later), but by asking your children to tell you about teams they've been on. Chances are excellent that the teams they really liked were effective teams, teams that accomplished something, and that those they didn't like were ineffective. The overall purpose of this discussion is to help your children understand that being a good team member is an important life skill, and one they can begin to learn through this talking activity.

We advise making the initial questions as open-ended as possible. For instance, "Tell me about one time when you were part of a team— whether it was in a club (like Students Against Drunk Driving), a sports team, or something else at school (band, student council, etc.)." Many kids clam up when asked to categorize things, so try to phrase the question in a way that will encourage them to just describe the team experience. Make clear your point in asking the question, even saying that there are no wrong answers. You just want to know what the team was like and what they liked and didn't like about being on it.

If the child can remember a really great team experience, be prepared for a long description! Kids will go into detail if they've ever been on a great team.

A friend's face lit up as she recalled the water-skiing team she joined when she was nine and stayed on until she was 16:

> That was a terrific team! Even though there was a president and a show director, it was up to the individual team members to make things happen. We put on two shows each week during the summer—and we practiced every day. Each show had a theme and different acts, with a storyline, costumes, music, dialog, and tricks. The different acts came together to tell a story.
>
> A different person took the lead for each act. It wouldn't have worked if five people had tried to lead, and it wouldn't have worked if no one had led. A girl who was a really good dancer usually made up the different dance rou-

tines and taught them to us. The group always decided who would perform in each act and who wouldn't. We all thought of ideas together: people would raise their hands and offer suggestions. Even though there were leaders assigned certain responsibilities, it was really democratic—we had the whole team, then a team within a team for the individual acts, and team spirit carried over into all of them.

Our goals were to have great acts showing high skill (from everyone), avoid falls (from anyone), win tournaments, and have fun. We really wanted to win—but we always had fun, too (just being together and working together on something important). We did fight about things at times, but when you have a show for 500 people the next night you work things out! To me, a nine-year-old, just feeling that I was part of something that important was fun—whether it was taking a small part in one act or taking the lead in another. Winning first place in the state tournament one year felt pretty darn good, too.

Research on teamwork and our friend's experience proves that on great teams the following things happen:

- People have clear goals, like putting on a great show and winning a state tournament.
- People have well-defined roles and responsibilities, from picking up skis to teaching skills to new members.
- Everyone is committed to achieving the goals—like wanting to practice *all day on Saturday* or as long as it takes to get it right.
- Roles, tasks, and people are flexible: for example, if the announcer is late, someone takes the microphone.
- Results are measurable; in competition, scores are assigned to each act.
- Planning is good and involves everyone.
- Everyone's contribution is valued; new members start by retrieving skis and winding ropes, but the whole team shows appreciation.
- Having fun is considered important.
- People confront and resolve conflicts. They don't hide them and they don't let them destroy the group.

- Team members trust each other.

- Clear, open communication is valued.

- The leader brings out the best in people without being bossy or domineering.

When your child talks about being on teams, the discussion will get into what worked well and what didn't work on your child's teams. After your child describes the teams he's been on, you can ask questions that will help him identify those qualities that are important in teamwork, like "That sounds like a really good team. What do you think made it so good?" If your child doesn't know what you mean, say something like "It sounds like everyone's ideas were appreciated. What else made it a good team?" or "It doesn't sound as though you enjoyed that team much. What might have made it better?"

When your child shows a good understanding of the characteristics of effective teams, it's time for practical training in how to be a team player.

Take a Ropes Course

The actual activity is to take a ropes course: it's a series of group problem-solving tasks designed to build strong teams and strengthen individual character. Ropes courses teach people how groups can be more effective, and how to be a good team player. Your whole family can participate, but an individual can sign up too.

Time: 30 minutes to an hour to talk about teams, two to three hours at the ropes course.

Venue: A local ropes course. (Google "ropes course" for locations.)

Equipment: Comfortable outdoor clothes; the ropes center will supply everything else you need.

Optional: Include another family or some of your children's friends.

In a ropes course, teams figure out how to overcome obstacles— some physical, some mental. You might be asked, for example, to put 10 people on a tire. Courses are physically and psychologically designed to give every member of the team the opportunity to be both the leader and a follower. It's left up to the group to decide each individual's role for every obstacle.

When you're ready to go to the ropes course, describe it to your kids as a fun outdoor activity: "Would you like to go on a ropes course? There will be a lot of outdoor activities that we will do as a team. You can bring friends."

> Courses are physically and psychologically designed to give every member of the team the opportunity to be both the leader and a follower.

If there isn't a ropes course near you, your community center or YMCA may have something similar—a series of outdoor activities for a group, designed to encourage contributions from each individual and show individuals how much fun it is to contribute to a team.

There are usually about 10 stations in a ropes course or similar outdoor game, each with an obstacle and a goal. These are typical station activities:

- Fit 12 people on a tire, within a certain amount of time. How are you all going to do that?
- Get 12 people up a rope wall and over the other side.
- Walk on a rope. To do this, you need to rely on and trust your teammates.
- Stand on top of a big tree stump, then fall back and have the other members of the group catch you. This is called the "trust fall."

As you perform each of these activities with your children, remember that the goal is to give them practice at being good team players—and that this includes being able to be both a leader and a follower.

How do you teach the traits that make people good team members? One way is by taking them out of their comfort zones,

> The goal is to give them practice at being good team players—and this includes being able to be both a leader and a follower.

albeit in a safe setting, and urging them to contribute in every way they can. They'll figure out how and what they can contribute in ways that may surprise you. The ropes course activities are planned to put everyone on the same playing field, with different leaders at every station. Each station is designed to test different skills and capabilities, so everyone can contribute. When you get to each station, let the kids figure out who's going to do what—this usually occurs naturally. However, if one sibling is dominating the exercise and seems to know all the right answers at each station, ask him or her to give someone else a turn. *Your role is to take a back seat, but not get out of the car* (metaphorically speaking).

Ropes courses are also designed to encourage praise and support. A lot of group encouragement goes on during the exercise—if the team members are working together effectively, each will just naturally encourage the others. This gives parents a break, too, because you won't have to be leading the effort. You're just as involved as the kids, and you can model the behavior of a team member who watches, listens, and praises.

Talk About It

At the end of some ropes courses, an employee might lead the group in a discussion of how the activity was for everyone. You can do the same type of review with your family team.

The 12 characteristics of effective teams we listed earlier will come up naturally, and kids who acted to improve cooperation, interject humor, or draw out more passive teammates will be praised as good team players. When your family is alone, you can talk about it some more—but let your kids do most of the talking and don't try to turn the conversation into a lecture or a test. Again, stay in the back seat but don't get out of the car. Ask questions and praise what your children did on the course as specifically as you can, as often as you honestly can. Point out how their actions

> Let your kids do most of the talking and don't try to turn the conversation into a lecture or a test.

152

made the experience better for everyone and ask what they would do differently next time.

Ideally, this will be one of many conversations your family has about teams. You can continue the discussion when you're watching sports (on TV or live) or whenever your kids are in group situations. When they're on teams that aren't working well, you can use the ropes course experience and the SMART Decision Pad to help them figure out what they can do to make the team better.

Notes

1. Baltasar Gracián, *The Art of Worldly Wisdom*. Translated by Joseph Jacobs. London and New York, Macmillan and Co., 1892. Cited in Lewis D. Eigen and Jonathan P. Siegel, *The Manager's Book of Quotations*. New York: AMACOM, 1989.

2. Alexandre Dumas, *The Three Musketeers*. Translated by Lowell Bair. Bantam Classics, 1984, reissue. New York: Bantam Classics, Bantam Dell Publishing Group, Random House, 2004. Cited in Lewis D. Eigen and Jonathan P. Siegel, *The Manager's Book of Quotations*. New York: AMACOM, 1989.

CHAPTER 17

BE A LEADER

People kept on saying, 'If only Nancy was here,' or 'What would Nancy have said about that?' The expedition itself seemed to have lost its point, until they agreed in council that it should be put off until she was well and able to come too. ... Nancy, mumps or no mumps, was the real leader of the expedition. The plans were hers.

—*Arthur Ransome,* Winter Holiday[1]

AN-DO KIDS LEAD WHEN IT'S appropriate to do so—and they're good at it. Kids who are leaders make things happen (they have ideas and initiative), make things fun (they're good planners and know how to generate enthusiasm), and make things important (they inspire other kids). But they can also be forceful if the situation calls for it. When a friend suggests doing something unethical, for example, a child who is a good leader and has a moral compass will put a stop to it, firmly and instantly. Kids can find the confidence and the right words to do this if parents have coached them.

So, no matter what your child ends up doing with his or her life, leadership skills are important. It's hard to stand up for what you believe in and accomplish anything that involves other people without leadership ability. In Chapter 16, ropes courses were cited as a way to teach kids to be team players as both followers and leaders. In this chapter, we offer two additional activities to help your child develop leadership skills:

- Start a business.
- Run a club.

Be a Leader

Time: For parents, a few minutes (lemonade stand) to several hours over time (more complex business or club). For kids, an afternoon (lemonade stand) to several hours per week (more complex business or club).

Venue: Anywhere you can talk (parental involvement), then anywhere your child is.

Equipment: Depends on the business and the club.

Start a Business

Even if your children have no desire to be entrepreneurs, starting a business is a great way to develop leadership skills that will stand them in good stead whatever they do. Also, many children think of starting a business on their own. We remember:

- The colleague, now the owner of a company, who started not a lemonade stand but lemonade concessions when he was 11. He hired several other kids to walk up and down the beach, with thermoses of cold lemonade and paper cups in knapsacks.

- A friend, now a university professor, who raised chickens and sold the eggs. His parents made him buy the chicken feed himself and he kept meticulous records. At the end of a year, he'd made enough to buy a new bicycle—not bad for a 10-year-old.

- Neighborhood children who walk dogs, shovel snow, and mow lawns in order to earn spending money.

Your child may well come to you with an idea for starting a business; alternatively, you could make a suggestion. One parent we know waited until his son asked for money, then suggested that he earn it with his own business. Either way, your role is to encourage and coach your child, whether he or she has to come up with an idea for a business or

> Your role is to encourage and coach your child, whether he or she has to come up with an idea for a business or needs help refining and executing an idea from you.

needs help refining and executing an idea from you. Use the SMART Decision Pad to help your child generate ideas, pick the best one, and make all the decisions that will follow.

How you will participate once these first decisions are made will depend on your child's age and resourcefulness. Younger children may need your help to figure out the answers to practical questions. For example, if a seven- or eight-year-old wants to set up a lemonade stand, you could ask these questions:

- "What do you need and how much will these things cost?"
- "How much will you charge?"
- "How much lemonade do you have to sell to make enough money to do what you want to do?"

A teenager with entrepreneurial interests and talents may want to start a real business—not a weekend lemonade stand, but an ongoing, profit-making, tax-paying enterprise. This requires research, groundwork, and planning; it's an activity for kids with drive, determination, and a certain amount of business knowledge.

Your role could range from being the occasional sounding board (for a budding entrepreneur, full of great ideas and energy) to being an active consultant (on the business plan, hiring, accounting, taxes) or business partner (investing in equipment). For example, the son of one client paid for his college education by selling telemarketing services. He recruited friendly, outgoing, assertive students from his dorm. Another example is a group of kids we know who noticed that retailers in their high-crime neighborhood weren't retaining the people who serviced appliances. So the kids got together and developed a business plan. First they persuaded the retailers to train *them* and then they negotiated service contracts, ultimately creating a profitable business.

Run a Club

As parents, we glow with pride when one of our children is elected officer of his or her class or a club. It shows peer approval and looks impressive on a college application. We tend to think that being elected class vice president proves a child is a leader. However, winning an election can show popularity, not necessarily leadership ability. What demonstrates leadership is accomplishing something *meaningful* through others' actions. Some students might make winning the election their goal, whereas go-getters use winning the election as an opportunity to lead people and make a difference.

Just an Officer	A Leader
As treasurer, kept accurate books and the club stayed within the annual budget.	As treasurer, computerized all records, initiated a fund raiser that doubled the budget, which permitted revamping the recreation center.
As vice president, conducted monthly meetings according to Robert's Rules of Order and organized annual election.	As vice president, initiated first class-wide diversity program, with monthly day-long exchanges with students from varying backgrounds.

Figure 17-1. An officer versus a leader

You can help your child make the distinction and rise to the occasion by emphasizing the importance of developing true leadership skills. When your child is elected to an office, encourage her to use the SMART Decision Pad with her team of officers. She might convene an initial meeting to establish clear, measurable goals for the year. Whatever the club's goals, coach her to lead her team in identifying the challenges, brainstorming possible solutions, evaluating options, etc. A plan will have to be developed for each goal, with your child deciding who will do what and with what timetable. For a major project, well-meaning adults (teachers, student advisors, parents) might offer to intervene and even try to take over. Encourage your child to do as much as she—and you—feel she can handle.

Larry Bossidy, retired CEO of Honeywell, and author of the groundbreaking books *Confronting Reality* and *Execution*, has nine boys. He used a unique way to help them develop leadership. "I traveled a lot, so I told one of my kids, 'I'm the official Head Coach and you're Assistant Coach. However, *you* will do most of the coaching. You'll be the one organizing practices, getting kids to games, handling parents who want their kid to play more, and 100 other things. If you need help, ask your brothers who have been assistant coaches in the past and ask me when you face a big challenge.' It worked out fine." This might be more of a "sink or swim" activity than you want for your child, but the Bossidy household was already wired for it. The boys had been in command of many situations before they were given the Little League team to coach.

If your child isn't in a club that offers leadership opportunities and has a strong interest in something that would make a good club, encourage her to start it. When she's enthusiastic about the opportunity, ask how she would do the following:

- Recruit friends who want to be in this club.
- Get approval from the administration.
- Establish a vision for the club and measurable goals.
- Recruit other members outside of her circle of friends.
- Handle finances.
- Achieve meaningful results.

- Resolve differences among officers and/or members.
- Build teamwork among the officers.
- Positively motivate the members.
- Train a successor.

You will be a sounding board for your child, helping *her* become a sounding board for others.

Starting a club and making it successful are important experiences for developing leadership skills, as long as well-meaning administration advisors or parents don't take over. Successful community clubs (arts, drama, scouting, Boys' and Girls' clubs, etc.) have adult leaders who instill resourcefulness in the kids. Instead of making decisions *for* kids, these adult leaders coach the kids to set their own goals, identify problems, solve problems, raise money, set rules, compose schedules, and evaluate success.

Kate shows "Zambian Exchange Club" t-shirt to Zambia's Minister of Tourism.

I (Kate) started the Zambian Exchange Club in high school. We exchanged letters with African students sharing environmental concerns. In its first year, the club sent 400 pounds of educational materials to Zambia and raised money to train a Zambian student in environmental education. The faculty advisor let me and the club's other officers figure things out. By the end of the next year, the club had gathered thousands of American and Zambian students' signatures on a petition asking the government of Zambia to put an end to poaching elephants.

After that, I was invited to Zambia to present the petition to a Cabinet Minister in person. My father went with me and we were both very surprised when we were invited to be on Zambian television the day after our arrival. We role-played the kinds of questions the interviewer would likely ask and then went to the *Good Morning Zambia* studio. Everyone at the studio was surprised when my father declined to be interviewed along with me, telling the program manager, "She did it all—I was just an observer. She should be the one you interview."

> Can-do kids blossom when parents coach them to make better and better decisions.

As with all the activities in this book, can-do kids blossom when parents coach them to make better and better decisions. Too many well-meaning parents give so much advice or do so much of the work that the children shrug their shoulders and think, "The club/business/science project/composition was really my mom's." Sorry if we sound like a broken record, but we remind you: to teach your child to be a can-do leader, use the SMART Decision Pad and enough patience that she, not you, is the leader.

Note

1. Arthur Ransome, *Winter Holiday.* Boston: David R. Godine Publisher, 1989.

CHAPTER 18

SPOT A WINNER,
SPOT A WHINER

Mrs. Gummidge did not appear to be able to cheer up. She took out an old black silk handkerchief and wiped her eyes; but instead of putting it in her pocket, kept it out, and wiped them again, and still kept it out, ready for use. ...

"I know what I am. I know I am a lonely, forlorn creature, and not only does everything go contrary with me, but that I'm contrary with everybody. Yes, yes, I feel more than other people do, and I show it more. It's my misfortune."

I really couldn't help thinking, as I sat taking all this in, that the misfortune extended to some other members of that family besides Mrs. Gummidge.

—*Charles Dickens,* David Copperfield[1]

"I AM THE MASTER OF MY FATE: I am the captain of my soul"[2] is how successful people feel. Psychologists would say they have an "internal locus of control." They feel in charge of their own lives, they take responsibility for their own feelings and behavior—and they don't blame other people or fate. They're winners. Losers tend to blame others, whine, feel like victims, and make themselves and everyone around them miserable.

Like Mrs. Gummidge in *David Copperfield*, losers expect everything to "go contrary."

In this chapter, you talk about winners and whiners with your child—not for very long, but just enough for them to see the difference between the two and the relevance to their happiness and success. Then you present the activity: you'll try to spot winners and whiners when you're out in public together. If you can't talk about what you notice at the time because the person might hear you, you can talk about them later.

Talking about other people as whiners might sound mean, but helping your children recognize when other people are acting like victims makes it easier for them to recognize when they themselves are behaving this way. And conversely, it will also help them recognize when they are acting like winners and motivate them to take more responsibility for their behavior.

In this chapter, we hope to enable you to make your child a winner. You will:

- Discuss the difference between winners and whiners.
- Spot winners and whiners.
- Convert those observations into a personal success platform.

Spot a Winner, Spot a Whiner

Time: Five or ten minutes to prepare in private, two minutes to do in public, another two to discuss. This is an activity that can be repeated often.

Venue: Out in public, wherever you are: in line at the grocery store, at a movie theater, in an airport, at an amusement park, and so forth.

Equipment: None.

Discuss the Difference Between Winners and Whiners

At a quiet time when you're both in the mood to talk, have a brief discussion about the difference between whiners and winners. You can make the distinction by describing them as follows:

Whiners are grown-ups or children who choose to complain and feel sorry for themselves instead of doing something to get what they want. They don't see their negative attitude as a choice, though; they think it's just how things are.

Winners are grown-ups or children who take responsibility for making good choices, for their attitudes, their behavior, and their goals. They decide what they want and try to be it or do it. They rarely blame other people—or fate.

The discussion will probably be more interesting if you give real-life examples that your children can relate to and ask your children to give or make up examples too. Or you can describe a situation and ask what a whiner would say and do and what a winner would say and do. Your children may surprise you by how aware of this distinction they already are, but just in case, here are some examples.

Winners Say	Whiners Say
"I messed up. Next time I'll ...."	"Why does this happen to me all the time?"
"I felt angry, I felt sad."	"He made me angry, he made me sad."
"I'd like to dress up as a cat this time."	"How come I always have to wear the bunny suit?"
"I can stick it out."	"I always get the short end of the stick."
"I could ...."	"There's nothing I can do about it."
"Isn't this great?"	"Woe is me!"
"Life is what I make it."	"My life sucks."
"Now that I don't have to clean out the stable every morning, I can ...." (take piano lessons, sleep later, spend the night at a friend's house ...)	"First Dad sells the pony. Then the turtle dies."
"I can do it."	"I can't do it."
"We'll get through this."	"This is such a problem."

Spot Winners and Whiners

When you're sure your children understand what you mean by winners and whiners, say something like "Next time we're out in public, let's see if we can find some whiners and some winners, based on this discussion that we've just had. It will be interesting to see what your take is on it and who you find." If you see one and your children don't react, you can discreetly point the person out by saying, "Did you see that?" or "Did you hear that?" If the person is still within hearing distance, discuss it later. After all, the purpose of this activity is to teach a very important life lesson. It's *not* to make fun of people or embarrass anyone.

Ask open-ended questions that encourage your children to describe in detail what they observed, then express their thoughts: "So what did you see? What was the person saying? Why was that person a whiner or a whiner?" What whiners are ultimately saying, though unintentionally, is that they *choose* to fail and to be unhappy. This activity shows your child that viewing situations negatively or positively *is a choice,* that they themselves can choose how they want to react in almost any situation. That's what winners do!

You may be surprised by how much your children have to say and how observant they are. Remember not to guide the discussion too much. See where they go with it—children are often far more perceptive than adults realize. Both of the whiners in the following stories were spotted by friends of ours when they were children.

One can-do kid who became a can-do adult remembers:

I was ten, my cousin was six, and we were at the cabin, having a nice lunch. … at least, everyone else thought it was a nice lunch. Mario didn't like it and he let everyone know it: "This tastes gross, this tastes disgusting, I can't eat this, I need a cookie …." On and on it went until lunch was over. He sulked and complained for the rest of the day, saying the meal had "ruined" his day.

Later, when the rest of us were on the dock, jumping into the lake with our inner tubes, he continued to sulk and complain. He really spun his own web of misery—or, as I phrased it to myself at the time, "Wow, Mario sure missed out on all the fun this afternoon because he was still sulking about lunch! Why didn't he just make himself a sandwich?"

People like Mario feel negatively about themselves and life in general. Mario unconsciously needed to be miserable, so if the lunch hadn't displeased him, the weather or something else would have. Mario was a whiner; a winner wouldn't have let a food he didn't like ruin his lunch, let alone his day!

Another friend remembers a scene at the family dinner table. Her mother had made tomato sauce with shrimp, but she'd been in a hurry and hadn't peeled the shrimp. The father took one bite and exploded, "(expletive deleted), Sally! This is like having peanut butter with the shells still on the peanuts!" The mother didn't say a word, she just looked really sad. Our friend was outraged. Between courses, she followed her mother into the kitchen. "Why don't you just say something back to him?" The mother sighed in a martyred way. "Oh, it wouldn't do any good," she said.

A winner might say something like this to her irate husband: "I'm really sorry I didn't shuck the shrimp. But we get unshucked shrimp all the time at the Red Lobster. Why don't I get towels and bowls so we can all shuck them ourselves? In other words, "Let's make the best of the situation"

Our behavior as parents is copied by our kids and to raise can-do children we must be winners, not whiners. What kind of example does the father's outburst and the mother's cowering set for their kids? If you make a mistake and act like a whiner in front of your kids, tell them later how you wish you had reacted, how a winner would have acted.

Praise your children whenever they act like winners. Whenever you're out in public (or even watching TV together), encourage your children to spot winners and talk about them. Have them describe winners in detail, so they truly understand the advantages in life of being "can-do" rather than "can't do."

One child told his parents at dinner that his friend's dad seems like a real winner. "When I was at Sameer's house last night, his dad told me that he loved his new job. Apparently he hated his old one and figured that getting an advanced degree would give him more options, so he spent three years attending night school, and he just graduated and has a better job now. Good for him for doing this! It must have been tough going to school and working, but he seems so much happier now. Sameer said that everyone in their family is happier as a result too."

When we take responsibility for anything in life, we feel happier because we're in control, not blaming other people and not feeling like a victim. When we have this winning attitude, we're more apt to seek out opportunities and try—in good times and bad. We don't shy away from the tough decisions. Remember:

Resourcefulness = Motivation x Decision Making

There is always something we can do. It takes wanting to (motivation) and figuring out what (decision making).

Perhaps that is the single most valuable lesson anyone can learn: "I control my feelings—nothing and nobody else can." It may be hard to accept that principle when you imagine people suffering huge losses or experiencing tragedies, but even in the very worst circumstances, as the coverage of national disasters shows, a real hero triumphs over adversity if only in his or her own mind.

Notes

1. Charles Dickens, *David Copperfield*. New York: Modern Library, Random House, 2000, p. 38.
2. William Ernest Henley, "Invictus," 1875.

CHAPTER 19

LOOK AHEAD,
PREVENT A PROBLEM

"We're as good as dead."

"Shh! Don't you worry, Gretel, I'll find a way to help us."

And as soon as the old folks had gone to sleep, he got up, put on his little coat, and slipped out. The moon was shining as bright as day, and the white pebbles that lay there in front of the house glittered like new silver coins. Hansel stooped over and put as many as he could into his pockets. . . .

[The next night, when they'd been left in the forest] Gretel began to cry and said, "How will we ever get out of the forest?" But Hansel comforted her: "Just wait awhile until the moon comes up, then we'll be able to find our way." And when the full moon came up, Hansel took his little sister by the hand and followed the pebbles that glittered like new silver coins and showed them the way.

—Jacob Grimm and Wilhelm Grimm, "Hansel and Gretel,"
The Complete Grimm's Fairy Tales[1]

EING ABLE TO LOOK AHEAD AND prevent a problem is a skill that can literally make the difference between life and death. That's probably why folk tales in all cultures teach children the importance of doing it. (In case you don't remember the story: by the end of "Hansel and Gretel," Gretel learned to plan ahead. In fact, her plan tricks the witch and saves both children's lives.)

Almost all the activities in this book teach children to think ahead—a skill that's key to making rational decisions. This activity makes a game out of anticipating problems and figuring out how to prevent them. It may also provide a safe, non-threatening way for your children (especially older children) to deal with problems that are too serious or too embarrassing for them to feel comfortable discussing directly.

In this chapter you will learn how to do the following:

- Introduce the game: everyone in your family will write down a real or hypothetical problem on a piece of paper and then fold it up.

- Play the game: each person picks a piece of paper and describes ways in which the problem could have been prevented.

- Discuss each solution together as a group. (If you suspect that an imaginary scenario is quite real, don't let on! Respect your child's privacy—unless your knowledge of your child tells you that he or she actually *wants* you to guess that it's real and help him or her talk about it.)

Look Ahead, Prevent a Problem

Time: 15 minutes to an hour.

Venue: Any place you can talk.

Equipment: Something to write with, at least four people.

Introduce the Game

Explain the game so that it sounds fun. Then, encourage your children to be really creative in thinking of problems and ways to prevent them. You, the parents, start the activity by describing a real or imaginary problem and suggesting ways to prevent it. Here's an example:

I'm a student, it's Sunday night and my big science project is not done and won't be done by Monday morning, when it's due. How could I have prevented missing the homework deadline?

- I could have found homework buddies who are good at my hard subjects, and we could have done our homework together over the phone. Maybe I could have helped them with their hard subjects that I'm good at in return. Had I done this, my homework wouldn't have piled up.

- I could have gotten into the habit of looking at my homework assignments on Friday night before dinner and deciding when I'm going to do them.

- I could have made a homework calendar and put it in the kitchen—and then written the day's (or the weekend's) homework on it while having my after-school snack.

As you describe hypothetical problems and ways to prevent them, be sure to think outside the box and come up with several solutions for each problem—and the more unexpected, the better. This will inspire your children to be creative when *they* are thinking of solutions. After you've done enough examples for the kids to understand what you mean by *preventing* problems, you can all take turns thinking of scenarios or for *solving* problems.

Simply introducing this activity from time to time tells your children you believe in solving problems, and frequently the best way to solve them is to *prevent* them.

How Could You Prevent These Problems from Happening?

- You and three other second-graders are on the playground, playing four-square. As usual, everyone is fighting about whose turn it is.

- You're playing soccer, a storm comes up, and you remember that you left the window open next to your computer.

- You and three new friends are playing gin rummy and—in the middle of the game—someone says aces are high and someone else says they're low.

- You wake up one morning and discover that your bike is gone.

- Some friends give a party while their parents are out of town and the house gets trashed.

- A friend told you he was going to cheat on a test. He did, and he got caught and suspended from school.

- You're on a diet to lose weight. You go to a party, you're starving, and you eat four pieces of pizza … and then you feel awful afterwards: guilty and stuffed!

You can use these situations to start the game or make up your own. Encourage your kids to first brainstorm and then analyze ways to prevent the problem scenarios from occurring. Learning to think ahead is the real goal of this game. It's fine to push your kids a little during the brainstorming and to keep at it until they come up with lots of ideas for preventing the problems from occurring. Remember that during the brainstorming phase of the SMART Decision Pad, even wild or silly ideas are OK. Analysis comes later, after you've thought of ideas. If you start analyzing and criticizing solutions before you've finished brainstorming, you may lose some good solutions. Analysis and feedback should come after creative thinking.

When kids get into this game, they sometimes find the activity so stimulating that they start talking about real situations troubling them. They may say the situations are real or they may present them as hypothetical or happening to friends. Whichever way they choose to bring them up, if you listen without judging, you'll be showing them that it's safe to talk about these topics with the family.

The game teaches your children to apply the SMART Decision Pad to their own lives by using it to identify real goals and options to avoid problems. No matter how tempted you may be to make judgments and provide answers, limit yourself to listening and coaching. Remember that the goal is for them to learn. Children who are encouraged to think ahead and prevent problems don't just help themselves; they often help other people too. A long-term practitioner of can-do child parenting suggested we interview his daughter Casey who walked us through how the SMART Decision Pad led her to the right decision (Figure 19-1).

In my freshman year of high school, a friend came to me and told me she had taken eight Advil. I asked her about it and she said she had a bad headache-but she seemed really depressed.	*The SMART Decision Pad was going through my mind.*
I felt uncomfortable asking this, but I did: "Were you doing it to hurt yourself or did you really have a headache?" "I really just had a headache." "Well, it's not normal to take that amount for a headache." At that, she got kind of mad and said, "Just don't tell anyone, I'm fine!"	*Study the situation.*
I thought about it. I was worried about her health. I considered the options:	*Make the goal clear: keep her healthy.*
Option 1: do not tell anyone. **Advantages:** ▪ loyal to friend ▪ she trusts me—she's happy **Disadvantages:** ▪ she might get sick ▪ this could lead to something more serious (next time it might be her mother's prescription sleeping pills, not Advil) ▪ I don't feel comfortable **Option 2:** tell an adult **Advantages:** ▪ she could get appropriate help ▪ someone with more experience can make the decision-I feel comfortable, relieved ▪ she's safe, she lives! **Disadvantages:** ▪ she doesn't trust me anymore ▪ she gets angry at me—she ends the friendship	*Assess various options.*

Figure 19-1. SMART Decision Pad in action (continued on next page)

I decided that even at the risk of losing a friend, some adult should know what had happened—so I told the school counselor, who told my friend's parents. It ended in her being taken out of school and put in a mental health facility.	*Realize the best options and do it.*
When she came back, she was bitter and angry with me. Our friendship deteriorated; we didn't hang out as much, but ultimately I was still glad I'd told someone, because she was alive even though we weren't as close as we had been. Sometimes the right decision doesn't have a completely happy outcome, but it's best.	*Take stock: evaluate how the SMART Decision Pad process worked.*

Figure 19-1. SMART Decision Pad in action (continued)

The SMART Decision Pad helped Casey think clearly, stay calm, and make a rational decision about a difficult situation; it brought clarity. Teaching children to think ahead really can save lives—that doesn't just happen in fairytales!

Note

1. Jacob Grimm and Wilhelm Grimm (Brothers Grimm), *The Complete Grimm's Fairy Tales*. Translated by Margaret Hunt and James Stern. Reissue edition. New York: Pantheon Books, 1976.

CHAPTER 20

VOLUNTEER

The beggar girl was still huddled up in the corner of the step.... Sara opened the paper bag and took out one of the hot buns, which had already warmed her own cold hands a little.

"See," she said, putting the bun in the ragged lap, "this is nice and hot. Eat it, and you will not feel so hungry."

The child started and stared up at her, as if such sudden, amazing good luck almost frightened her; then she snatched up the bun and began to cram it into her mouth with great, wolfish bites.

"Oh, my! Oh, my!" Sara heard her say hoarsely, in wild delight. "Oh my!"

Sara took out three more buns and put them down.

The sound in the hoarse, ravenous voice was awful.

"She is hungrier than I am," she said to herself. "She's starving." But her hand trembled when she put down the fourth bun. "I'm not starving," she said—and she put down the fifth.

— *Frances Hodgson Burnett,* A Little Princess[1]

WE REMEMBER READING ABOUT an expensive dinner sponsored by Oxfam, the relief organization, in England. The organization gave a dinner to dramatize world hunger; guests were told that they would receive either a multi-course meal or empty plates, but wouldn't know in advance which they would get. Donors were to sit at tables with other adult donors, and their kids would sit at tables with other kids. At the adult tables, everyone seemed uncomfortable as those who got full plates ate and those who had empty plates watched. At the children's tables, everyone shared! The kids just heaped food onto each other's plate. Parents later explained that their kids didn't "get it," that some at each table were supposed to go hungry that night to better understand hunger. But the kids said their parents didn't "get it," because a lot of world hunger was preventable if nations with food shared. As they say, "out of the mouth of babes."

World politics aside, every parent can cite examples in which their kids were selfish and when they were generous. And most would like their kids to be more generous. By modeling generosity, parents can inspire their kids to volunteer their time to help others, and to be generous. Most children will enjoy the two activities in this chapter:

- An act of kindness that the whole family brainstorms and executes together.
- Encouragement and discussion of little things you each can do for other people every day.

Volunteer

Time: Half an hour to discuss and plan, 30 seconds to several hours to do.

Venue: In public; depending upon what you decide to do.

Equipment: Depending upon what you decide to do.

In a self-absorbed, selfish society, doing things for someone else enhances us all. Being aware of other people's conditions and needs, not just your own, gives us a better understanding of people in general. Acts of kindness also build self-esteem and are rewarding and fun.

Volunteer as a Family

We suggest being obviously exuberant about this activity. Talk to your children about altruism and the importance of giving your time and using your imagination to help other people. One father we know announced it like this: "We're going to do a family volunteer project. Here's the fun part: you kids get to decide what we'll do. What kinds of things would you be interested in doing? Would you like to work with people, plants, or animals?"

Begin with broad categories like that and then just let the kids ramble on with different kinds of ideas—brainstorm! And remember: when you're brainstorming, no idea is too wild or crazy or silly. Use a version of the SMART Decision Pad, as a group, to pick the best idea. Here's how it goes, step by step:

- Brainstorm all kinds of ideas.
- Discuss the pros and cons of each.
- Pick one.
- Make a plan: figure out who's going to do what, making sure that everyone has a role and, if the activity is complicated, schedule it.
- Do it.
- Talk about it afterwards.

What makes this meaningful and interesting is that the family comes up with the idea: you're not just giving money to an organization or attending meetings. Thinking of the idea yourselves and seeing it through will be a fun, inspiring activity for the whole family, from the brainstorming to the discussion and bonding memories afterwards. You'll also be giving your children the feeling that they are doing something that matters, something important.

Families have:

- Made and delivered dinner to someone new in the neighborhood.
- Performed chores for an elderly neighbor.
- Babysat a single mother's kids for the afternoon and evening so she could do errands.

- Cleaned up a garbage-filled empty lot and planted flowers there.
- Collected *good* children's books—books the children themselves liked—and sent them to a library in Guyana.
- Collected used computers and sent them to Nigeria.
- Walked dogs (as a family) for the SPCA shelter. The parents, who knew their children well, made a rule beforehand—no matter how much we like the dogs, we aren't bringing any home with us.
- Drawn pictures for an assisted living center and then presented them to the residents and helped hang the pictures.
- Made cookies for the residents of an assisted living center, sang carols there, and then stayed to chat and drink cocoa.

Your children may come up with ideas that are generous, but impossible to implement; encourage their resourcefulness to get them thinking of ways to adapt these ideas and make them doable. For example, if a young child says, "I want to build a house for someone!" You might say, "Well, that's a nice thought but not realistic: building a house is a big, expensive project. But there are Habitat for Humanity projects; would you like to go online and find one we could all do? Or maybe you could think of something we could do as a family in one afternoon."

Plan it so that everyone, even the youngest child, contributes. With a little thought, every member of the family, no matter how young, can do something. For example, if you're all planting trees, even a three-year-old can participate by patting down the dirt or passing tools. Ideas can grow in remarkable, exciting ways too, like the Zambian Exchange Club we mentioned in Chapter 17.

Do Something for Someone Every Day

More informally, you and your children can each do something for someone else, no matter how small, every day, and talk about it at dinner. Good deeds can be *very* small but very meaningful.

When challenged to describe his good deed for the day, 16-year-old Liam said, "I was getting a hamburger and the kid ahead of me in line was embarrassed because he found he didn't have enough money for a

Coke. I said I'd pay for it. No big thing, but the kid really appreciated it, and it made me feel good." Good deeds are sometimes spontaneous, like helping grandpa to his feet.

One way to encourage your children to do something nice for someone might be to ask, "If someone had done something nice for you today, what would that have been?" If your child can't think of anything or doesn't know what you mean, give examples from your own childhood. Think of a time when a small act of kindness by someone else made a big difference to you and tell about it. You can make this into a little story. Or you could just list simple things:

- Helping someone pick up groceries after their bag broke.
- Holding a door for someone who has a lot of packages.
- Running over to someone who fell and scraped her knee and asking, "Can I help?"

When your children understand, make a pact: "We'll do one or more good deeds tomorrow and share them at dinner."

On a flight, I (Brad) sat next to a woman in her 40s. During the flight, she had helped older passengers stow their luggage overhead, retrieved a dropped pen, offered to switch meals with someone who wanted the meal she had chosen (and there were no more of that selection left), and was unusually nice to the flight attendant. Intrigued, I said, "I notice you're doing a lot for complete strangers." She replied, "Actually, I'm being selfish—I like myself more when I show 10 little acts of kindness every day. My parents taught me that."

If your children get into the habit of showing one "little act of kindness" daily and you praise them for it and share your act for the day, your can-do kids might become a little more caring, interested in others, and generous. They might become a little happier for volunteering to help someone and they will earn the respect of others for being a nice person.

Note

1. Frances Hodgson Burnett, *A Little Princess*. New York: Charles Scribner's Sons, 1938.

CHAPTER 21

LEARN TO BUDGET

"At last Mr. Micawber's difficulties came to a crisis and he was arrested early one morning and taken to the King's Bench Debtor's Prison. He solemnly encouraged me, I remember, to take warning by his fate; and to observe that if a man had twenty pounds a-year for his income, and spent nineteen pounds nineteen shillings and six-pence, he would be happy, but that if he spent twenty pounds one he would be miserable."

—*Charles Dickens,* David Copperfield[1]

AS MANY PEOPLE KNOW, to their sorrow, being unable to manage money is a real disadvantage in life. The best way to help your children avoid that fate is to teach them to budget, and more importantly, to live within a budget. Managing money sensibly and realistically can become second nature. Begin by showing them how to budget and discuss the problems people face when they spend impulsively and thoughtlessly. If they learn this lesson while they're young, they're less likely to get into financial trouble later. In this activity you will:

- Have your children budget, shop, and pay for a meal, with cash.
- Require your kids to live within their budget.

> **Learn to Budget**
>
> **Time:** 15 minutes at home planning, one hour in the grocery store.
>
> **Venue:** At home, in the grocery store.
>
> **Equipment:** Something to write with, cookbook, cash.

Budget for a Meal

The first step in this activity is to discuss what a budget is and why it's important to have one. When your children have an understanding of the concept, suggest that they learn about budgets by budgeting for a meal.

Ideally, your children will do this activity together. However, if they are very competitive—or just fight a lot—each of them can do it separately and see who can prepare the best meal on the budget. Either way, they will have a fixed amount to spend; this amount will be stipulated in advance and handed over in cash: "This is how much there is to spend. What meal can you make for that or less?" The children will plan the meal, go to the store and buy the groceries, and, if they want, prepare the meal too. The only rigid requirement here is that the children absolutely stick to the budgeted amount—you won't give them more money! This is a first effort at learning to live within a budget, so be firm. If their groceries are even a few cents over the limit, they have to put something back. That's how budgets work—or should work—in real life.

You can also set other parameters—that the meal must contain a protein plus two vegetables, for instance—but the kids choose what the meal will be within those parameters. Older children cook it; younger children help you cook it. The main point is for them to plan and shop for it, staying within the agreed-upon budget. Have them make a shopping list and estimate (or guess) how much things will cost. Seeing what items really do cost is part of the lesson here. Although the kids will do the shopping and pay for the groceries, parents can chime in during planning and at the store too, saying things like "Are you sure you want to do that? It takes three hours to cook" or "Why don't you read the directions on that label before you decide?"

Allow three or four times the amount of time you usually allot to grocery shopping for this activity—debating all this is a lengthy process and part of the learning experience. We also suggest that you let your child push the shopping cart. If you have a toddler, leave him or her at home. Toddlers require a lot of attention in grocery stores. This activity will be more pleasant if you're not distracted and can focus on the child or children learning to live within their shopping budget.

Require Kids to Live Within Their Allowance Budget

Putting expenses on paper is part of good money management, and can help prepare a child for eventually getting an allowance and living within the allowance budget. Let your children pick out little notebooks they can carry around with them and use to write down exactly what they spend. If they are computer-savvy, set them up with a simple program and have them track expenses on a computer. You can look at their expenses together and talk about them or the children can keep them private. If that idea doesn't appeal to your children, ask them if they can think of other ways to keep track of their money. When they can accurately record their expenditures, they can learn to "live" within their budget.

Many children receive an allowance for doing household chores and many are paid for additional household projects, so they'll have more spending money. With the previous parts of this activity completed, it's time to *require* your children to not overspend. If the allowance pays for movies and then the child runs out of money, there is no movie. If the bike costs $150 and your child has saved $125, you *don't* throw in an additional $25 and don't give a loan. This teaches kids to be resourceful in budgeting by experiencing the consequences of overspending, under-planning, or not working enough. When kids run short on cash, encourage a can-do solution. When one child we know couldn't go to the movies with her friends because she'd spent her allowance, she invited everyone over to her house to watch a video and eat homemade pizza.

Children eight years of age and older can be expected to take increasing responsibility for living within their means. Whether they earn some or all of their spending money, kids need to make choices. Eight-year-olds can do chores and earn money to spend as they wish. Teens can have budgets for clothes, books, gasoline (for driving), and recreation. Our favorite allowance system has kids awarded half their money for performing ordinary chores (making their bed), and half for projects (painting garage floor). Their expenditures must be two-thirds for clothes and entertainment (iPod, bike), one-sixth for savings, and one-sixth for charity. The savings component leads to learning to invest (Chapter 22), and the charity component opens up plenty of opportunities for resourcefulness in giving (already covered in Chapter 20).

Of the more than 6,500 executives Brad has interviewed, 90 percent worked as pre-teens and teenagers, and were required to live within budget constraints. They learned to appreciate values of hard work, frugality, and resourcefulness. Not bad lessons!

Note

1. Charles Dickens, *David Copperfield*. New York: Modern Library, Random House, 2000, p. 156.

Invest Early

What do we mean by "investor"? The term will be used in contradistinction to "speculator." An investment operation is one which, upon thorough analysis, promises safety of principal and an adequate return. Operations not meeting these requirements are speculative.

—Benjamin Graham, The Intelligent Investor[1]

IN THIS CHAPTER, OUR INTENT IS not to advise you on investing, but to suggest ways you can teach your children to become financially responsible and eventually maybe financially independent. With Social Security in jeopardy and one-fourth of baby boomers turning 60 having less than $1,000 in savings, investing is becoming increasingly important. This activity is for children old enough to live within a budget and understand the concept of putting money to work and making it grow. It will definitely appeal to children who are already very interested in money, and may be a new and interesting idea even to those who are not.

It's easy for adults to grasp the benefits of being financially independent: to be free to do what you want with your time, to be able to work at what you love, when and where you want. But even children who don't or can't think this far ahead may see the benefits of being able to, say, buy a car by the time they graduate from high school—simply by investing. If this sounds far too good to be true, give them the book *The Teenage Investor* by Timothy Olsen,[2] who did just that. In this activity, you will:

- Talk about the benefits of saving and investing, and about the "magic" of compound interest.
- Let your child research, choose, and track a hypothetical investment.
- Talk about what you both learned.

Invest Early

Time: 30 minutes to an hour for the initial discussion.

Venue: Any place you can talk quietly and, if you want to do the Web part of the activity, connect to the Internet.

Equipment: Computer connected to the Internet (optional), books (optional).

Talk to Your Child About Saving and Investing, and the Magic of Compound Interest

In Chapter 21, suggestions were offered for how to talk to kids about spending within limits. This chapter adds to that foundation some thoughts on what Americans don't do enough of: saving and investing. The main message is to save and invest *early in life* and you'll be financially a lot better off than if you start later. Why? Because of the magic of compounding.

Albert Einstein said the most powerful force in the universe is compounding. The idea that money itself can make money may or may not be a new idea to your child, but we believe the concept of compound interest is important. You can either explain the concept yourself, by using the ideas below or going to a Web site, or give your child a book written for young people. The easiest way to explain it to kids is with examples—you can use a paper and pencil, actual coins, poker chips, or Monopoly® money. Whatever you use as examples, put this idea into your own words.

"Your money earns money—that's the difference between investing and saving. If you put $100 in a piggy bank, at the end of the year, you have $100. If you put that same $100 into a bank that pays 5 percent interest, at the end of a year you have $105—$100 plus $5 interest. If you leave the money there, at the end of the next year you have $110.25:

> The idea that money itself can make money may or may not be a new idea to your child, but we believe the concept of compound interest is important.

$105 (amount at beginning of year 2) + $5.25 (the 10 percent interest) = $110.25. So how much would you have at the end of the third year?"

You can set up the problem for your child or just do the third year too: "$110.25 (amount at beginning of year 3) + $5.51 (5 percent interest) = $115.76. Want to figure out what it would be for the next year? And your money keeps growing: by the end of 7.2 years it will have doubled."

Once your child has the basic idea, you can go to any large investment firm's Web site and play with some numbers. They will have tools galore, with fancy graphics and tables that allow kids to plug in numbers and see compound interest at work. (After all, these companies want you to invest your money, so they put a lot of effort into making the ideas accessible and even exciting.) We can recommend www.LFG.com. The investment returns calculator on this site makes it easy to run scenarios for different assumptions: amount of investment, rate of return, number of years invested.

Some Web sites also illustrate the idea with dramatic stories. Or you can just tell the kids one yourself. For example, imagine twin brothers who each inherit $5,000 at age 10. One spends the money. The other invests it in securities that pay 10 percent; in 56 years, by the time he's 66, he has $1,039,825.28. He's a millionaire! His twin brother realizes when he's 20 that he hates his job and is not saving very much. He decides that *he* should start investing—and so he takes $5,000 that he's managed to save and invests it in exactly the same investments his brother chose. But by the time he's 66, after his investment has been earning interest for 46 years, he has only about $400,000. That may seem like a lot, but waiting 10 years to get smart enough to invest costs him about $600,000.

The fact that $5,000 can grow to $1 million may seem like magic. I (Brad) have interviewed hundreds of people who became millionaires saving 20 percent of their income and investing conservatively. And, they were not geniuses!

Or maybe your child would rather read and absorb this information at his own pace. If so, the book we mentioned earlier by Tim Olsen, *The Teenage Investor,* is a great choice because it is drawn from the author's own experience investing as a child. Tim bought his first share of stock when he was in second grade and wrote this book when he was 13. He is now a seasoned investor who's been on CNBC and in *Mutual Fund Magazine* and on Morningstar.com. He walks kids through the basic ideas and then shows them how to open a low-cost investment account that—in his case—was worth $25,000 after six years.

Choose and Track a Hypothetical Investment

Investing, as opposed to speculating, is the result of research and rational thinking, not wild guesses. Investments, even carefully chosen investments, can lose money as well as make money, and the greater the potential gain, the greater the potential loss. The best way to learn is to practice investing by choosing different investments and then see how they do over time.

> Investing, as opposed to speculating, is the result of research and rational thinking, not wild guesses.

Choosing an investment is another way of using the SMART Decision Pad: your child can define a goal, look at options, and evaluate the pros and cons of each. Most investing Web sites have questionnaires your child can use to learn, but most of these are *not* designed with children in mind, so you may want to be there, answering questions about risk tolerance and the like.

The fun in learning about investing for most kids comes in setting up a hypothetical portfolio, which can consist of any investments from a single stock, bond, or mutual fund to a complex mix of 20 or more. Web sites like Morningstar.com offer these for free. Your child can "buy" them all and then check the Web site from time to time for charts, reports, and news stories to keep track of how they're all doing. Some sites will send e-mails or messages to cell phones when the prices go up or down more than a certain specified amount. Tracking investments over time is much easier now than it used to be, without the Web—and for some children, a lot more fun. Teenagers making real or hypothetical investments can use these tools to analyze risk, change allocation, and play with all sorts of investments.

If your child is not interested in the Web—and some children aren't—you can do the same thing by choosing stocks and bonds from *The Wall Street Journal* or any other publication that follows the markets. Then you can check them together periodically or, if you

> The fun in learning about investing for most kids comes in setting up a hypothetical portfolio.

want to be really old-fashioned, make a chart by hand and plot the price daily or weekly.

I (Kate) remember doing this in grade school, when our fifth-grade class picked stocks to follow and found it surprisingly fun. We picked 10 stocks (discussing them all as a group, which was fun, too), gave each one a different color, and plotted them with daily prices from *The Wall Street Journal*. Some stocks did well, others not. I think we learned the most from failures, like putting too much money in one stock that flopped.

How early can a child learn about investing? A Smart Parenting reader sent the following stock chart, showing that his "brilliant" five year old had earned a 25 percent return in three months. After a discussion of how businesses made money, the father asked, "What do all the kids want for their birthday?" The five-year-old said, "Spiderman stuff!" So, he bought the stock of Marvel Entertainment, the company that made "Spiderman stuff." More than a few investors have sensed when to buy into a fad, but of course they need to sense when to sell, too. If this five-year-old continues investing, he'll learn many valuable lessons by the time he has real money to invest.

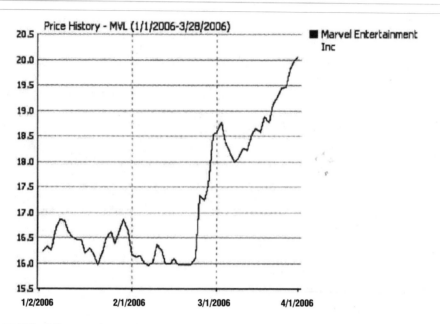

Price History - MVL (1/1/2006-3/28/2006)

■ Marvel Entertainment Inc

Talk About It

One of the most valuable parts of this activity is the discussions over time. For example, after your child has seen how his investments have performed, ask questions:

- "What did you learn?"
- "What would you do differently next time?"
- "What did you like best?"

Through these discussions, your child may learn to be more cautious, diversify investments, sell before a fad (Spiderman?) declines, or maybe to take more risks! Managing money prudently is one mark of a happy, successful adult, so even a little learning in this complicated field will be helpful to a child. Ninety-five percent of American adults regret not having saved when they were younger. The more parents educate their children about money and the financial security from saving and investing while they are young, the better off they will be as adults.

Notes

1. Benjamin Graham, *The Intelligent Investor.* 4th revised edition. New York: Harper Collins Publishers, 1973.

2. Timothy Olsen, *The Teenage Investor: How to Start Early, Invest Often, and Build Wealth.* New York: McGraw-Hill, 2003.

Chapter 23

Stay Calm, Cool, and Collected (No Matter What)

"There is nothing either good or bad, but thinking makes it so."
—*William Shakespeare,* Hamlet, Act II, Scene 2[1]

THE MEDIA HAVE BOMBARDED US with frightening statistics about how much stress is on kids and how poorly many cope with it—drugs, alcohol, promiscuous sex, violence, depression, and even suicide. If you think your children's stress levels, or their ways of coping with them, may be seriously hurting them, see Appendix B for helpful resources (including when to seek professional help). This chapter helps you coach your children to deal with stress.

Not all stress is harmful. The excitement of playing sports, performing in a concert, acting in a play, enjoying a birthday party, or getting an A on an important test is actually positive stress. A child who is never stressed may be a child who is never willing to try anything new. So we don't advocate severely limiting your children's exposure to stress. What we advocate is coaching your children to make smart choices so they get better and better at anticipating and avoiding situations that result in harmful stress. In that sense, almost every activity in this book deals with stress prevention.

When your children experience stress, we want them to cope with it constructively. In this chapter, you help your kids do that. The chapter shows you how to help children find ways to calm themselves down in stressful situations, think through what to do, and make the best of it.

> Not all stress is harmful. A child who is never stressed may be a child who is never willing to try anything new.

We believe that *we* are often our biggest sources of stress—not because of what happens to us, but because of how we react to what has happened. Fortunately, we can choose how we think and feel about any situation we're in.

A common example is passengers in line at the airport after their flight has been cancelled. Everyone has been inconvenienced; not everyone is negatively stressed. Some people yell and scream (sometimes to the point of being denied a flight), some complain, some fume silently; and some make the best of the bad situation. They do their yoga breathing exercises, figure out how to get to their destination another way, make phone calls, or read. We're not saying it's *easy* to react that calmly and constructively, but we are saying that it's possible. And we know from our own experience that the effort we put into reacting calmly takes a lot less out of us than getting stressed and staying that way.

> The effort we put into reacting calmly takes a lot less out of us than getting stressed and staying that way.

So how can you teach your children to stay calm, no matter what the provocation? In this chapter we recommend two things:

- Learn the physical signs of stress, so you can recognize them in your kids and coach your kids on how to recognize them too.
- Brainstorm as a family to find healthy ways to manage stress. Preventing excessive stress may not always be possible (and is covered in other chapters: everything we say in Chapter 19, "Look

191

Ahead, Prevent a Problem," may apply to stress!); so here we concentrate on dealing with it in healthy ways.

> ### Stay Calm, Cool, and Collected (No Matter What)
>
> **Time:** One hour, approximately.
>
> **Venue:** At home.
>
> **Equipment:** Flipchart or big piece of poster paper, magic markers. Optional: books, videos.

These are important activities. Surveys indicate that excessive stress accounts for 80 percent of all visits to the doctor's office and that nearly 100,000,000 Americans suffer from stress-related illness.[2] When parents feel stressed out they may pass it on to their kids. And these days, chances are that your children are stressed, too, whether you are or not. So this activity, more perhaps than many of the others in the book, is for parents and children alike. And you will want your child to take stress-prevention and -reduction skills into adulthood.

Prevent Stress

All of the activities in this book help create can-do kids who become can-do adults, and in our experience can-do people *can* get their stress levels under control. We have one sidenote to this broad generality regarding prevention: Some of your children's stress may even have been inadvertently caused by your overbooking and overscheduling their day. If you'd rather prevent stress than manage it, start by looking at your children's schedule.

Learn Signs of Stress

Many children are stressed without knowing it or being able to express it in words. Children may not have as many words for their feelings as we do and can be very inarticulate, especially about things that they feel deeply and intensely. Sometimes problems and reactions erupt emotionally. Sometimes they emerge as a lack of focus, failing to think clearly, or being easily distracted. Usually kids experience stress physically. And it's up to you to spot the physical signs and then take action! Grinding teeth, clenching or tensing muscles, and unexplained pains can all be signs of stress. Of course, pain can also be a sign of illness, but if your doctor can't find a physical cause, stress may be the culprit. If, for example, your child is having trouble sleeping, is suffering frequently from stomach aches or headaches, is wetting the bed, or is eating much more or much less than usual and your doctor doesn't detect illness, your child may be under some heavy stress and experiencing it physically.

For example, our colleague Lindsey remembers:

In second grade, my best friend got scarlet fever and was out of school for a long time. After awhile I started having stomach aches and headaches. I went to the nurse's office every day for a week and a half, telling them about these symptoms, but nothing was going on that they could see. I remember an adult saying, "Maybe you want to be sick like your friend—to get out of school and be home." I thought, "They don't think that my pain is real."

I remember them kind of laughing when I would come in, and that made me feel worse—as though I was doing something wrong. But I really did have stomach aches and headaches! I became hyper-vigilant of things around me. My Dad going on trips bothered me, the teacher yelling at another student scared me—little things that didn't normally bother me started to upset me (a sign of stress, I now know).

One person who really helped was my mother. She never once got mad at me. When I called from school asking to be taken home, she'd say things like "I'm sorry you're not feeling well. Can you stick it out a little bit longer?"

If she did come pick me up, she would ask me about different situations—and finally she thought to ask me about my sick friend, "Do you think about Melanie a lot?" I said I did. She had a hunch and started asking different questions about different feelings and finally I said, "Is Melanie going to die?"

I didn't know what scarlet fever was. I never asked about it. But I was terrified that my best friend was going to turn bright red and die!

My mother got it. She said, "Oh no, Lindsey, they have cures for this, the doctors are taking good care of her, and the nurses are taking good care of her. Do you want to talk to her at the hospital? We can call her as soon as we get home."

"Oooh, you can do that? I didn't even know they had phones in hospital rooms!"

With this combination of talking to me, listening to me, asking me questions, and most of all not blaming me, she figured out the cause of my problems— and lo and behold, my stomach aches and the headaches immediately stopped!

> We often hear adults saying things like "Stop whining." These types of comments are rarely helpful.

We often hear adults saying things like "Stop whining" or "Quit complaining about your stomach" and "You don't really have a headache." Sensitively noting signs of stress is a lot more helpful.

Make Yourself Calm

Many excellent books and videos describe the signs of stress in detail[3] and teach medically tested techniques to manage it safely and effectively. Below we briefly describe a few of our favorite techniques. We encourage you to learn them and then teach them to your children.

1. **Visualization.** With this technique, you think of a place that you find very comforting, imprint it on your brain, and then visit it when you feel stressed.[4] Really try to picture the place: the more vivid and specific your vision is, the more likely you are to remember it when you are stressed and the more effective it will be. So ask the following questions of your children to help them define and picture their "comfort scene"—and have them write down answers if they can:

   - "What is one place or scene in life that makes you feel at ease or calm?"

   - "What kinds of things can you smell there?"

   - "What do you see?" (Ask follow-up questions.)

   - "What do you hear?"

- "What are your hands touching? What are you sitting or lying or standing on? How does your body feel there—are you hot, cold, dry, wet?"
- "Are you eating anything? What does it taste like?"
- "What does the air feel like?"
- "Is anyone there with you? Who? What are they doing?"

Children find this activity fun, easy, and helpful. We know one seven-year-old who came up with it by himself. He didn't call it "visualization." He didn't use the word "stress." He just said, "When I'm nervous I feel icy all over. So, I take a minute by myself, close my eyes, and think of being in my bedroom warm and cozy. It makes me feel a little better."

As you do this activity with your children, encourage them to come up with a name for their stress-free place. (Some kids call it "my happy place," "a good place to go," or "comfort scene.") Then help them remember it with questions. When they have it handy in their head, they can call upon it naturally and instantly when they need to calm themselves down in stressful situations.

2. **Use positive self-talk.** The key here is to make up phrases and to speak them in a voice that *they* find calming or comforting. If you teach your children this technique, you might ask them to begin by picturing someone they find calming and comforting, and then imagining that person's voice speaking those phrases. Some children picture characters from books or movies—the Good Witch of the East waving her wand or a Gandalf-like wizard offering reassurances like these:

> The key here is to make up phrases and to speak them in a voice that *they* find calming or comforting.

- "Everything's going to be all right."
- "You can get through this."
- "Take it easy."
- "This will go away."

- "You'll be home soon."
- "Calm down."
- "Just breathe."

The positive self-talk statements don't have to be this philosophical or generic or bookish. One child we know pictured Davy Crockett cocking his rifle and taking aim! "I'm not going to shoot anyone," she said. "It just makes me feel like no one can scare me." Or they picture themselves at their best and say, "I'm going to be OK" or "I'm calm, cool, and collected."

Your children can choose whatever statements they want: the only rule is that it should be something that's their own. Some children may blank out when asked what they can say to calm themselves, but can think of plenty to say when the question is "What would you say to your friend to calm her down?" Once they've answered you, suggest, "Now say it to yourself."

3. **"Take 10."** This is good for older children who have anger issues. I (Brad) have worked with over 500 executives who had anger control issues and the technique that worked best when anger was rising is this:

   - Take one deep breath.
   - Leave the situation for 10 minutes—get something to drink, go to the washroom, or say, "I'm getting emotional, so let's take a 10-minute break."

   This is like the old "count to 10 rule," and research on anger control shows that it works.

4. **See the lighter side of it.** This isn't for everyone, but some people find it helpful to make light of the problem. Here's an example. When a class of yoga students was practicing an exercise and someone complained about pain, the yoga teacher said, "We don't call it 'pain' in yoga class—we call it a *sensation.*" Many students laughed—and this helped everyone grin and bear it. In the same spirit, we call difficult situations or people "challenges" or laugh at the idea of our "happy place," but go there anyway!

5. Brainstorm your own ways of managing stress. In this activity, you all think of good and bad ways to react to stress. (It may help to think of specific situations.) Take a sheet of poster paper or flip chart, divide it in half vertically, and then ask each person to write down a healthy way of handling stress and an unhealthy way. You're brainstorming, so *all* ideas are OK to write down. The only rule is that you take turns and each participant has to put down both a healthy and unhealthy way when it's his or her turn.

If your children don't know the word "stress" or you aren't sure if they understand what it is, begin by talking about it in words they can understand. You can describe times they seemed to be stressed. You can make stressed-out faces and gestures and ask them to do so, too. You can solicit examples from them by asking them to describe times when they felt nervous and uncomfortable. You can give them sentences to finish:

- "When the teacher calls on me and I don't know the answer, I ...." (Ask them to show you with their bodies what they do or tell you how they feel.)
- "When I am about to take a test, I ...."
- "When it's my turn to dive off the high dive, I ...."
- "When I get lost, I ...."

Your knowledge of your child will dictate the examples—and this should be about them, not about you. Use your own examples only for things that affect them directly. You can also encourage kids to talk about things you or other adults do that make them stressed. This gives kids a safe way to talk about things adults do that really bother them.

When you're ready to do the activity, give examples of what you mean by a healthy way and an unhealthy way. Think of a common situation. For example, you and the children are late for school.

Unhealthy way to respond. You shout, "Hurry up, get your stuff, we're late!" Maybe you swear and start throwing the coats and backpacks, too. By the time all of you are in the car, someone is crying and everyone is upset.

Healthy way to respond. You take a few deep breaths to calm down and then say in a calm, quiet voice, "Would you please get your things? We need to leave as soon as you do that, because we're running late." When all of you are in the car, you all brainstorm about how you can get out the door earlier. Maybe by setting the alarm 15 minutes earlier, maybe by laying out your clothes the night before, maybe by making the lunch the night before and putting it in the fridge ...

The healthy and unhealthy ways to cope don't have to have stories attached; just the behavior is enough. For example, blowing up at someone is an unhealthy way of handling stress; talking calmly about the problem is a healthy way. Hunching your shoulders is an unhealthy way; stretching them is a healthy way. Going for a walk is a healthy way; turning to alcohol is an unhealthy way.

When everyone has the idea, people take turns writing things down. The parents and the kids are involved. When it's your turn, you go up and write something down. (Children too young to write get to pick someone to write their idea for them.) It's quite amazing what kids come up with during this activity. You will end up with a long list of healthy and unhealthy ways to cope with stress; then you can use the SMART Decision Pad to help each child pick some that will work for him or her.

We incorporate brainstorming in many of the activities in this book because every time your family brainstorms, your children get better and better at it. The act of brainstorming is calming because people are doing something natural and constructive. With practice, kids are more likely to use it and the SMART Decision Pad when there is a crisis—and that is the time when evaluating the options rationally can make a big difference in their lives. They will need you to coach them at first, but eventually they will be able to calm down, brainstorm, and evaluate options on their own. Instead of acting out at home or blowing up at a teacher, a child who has done this activity will think, "I'll count to 10 and cool down now, and talk to Mr. Jones

> The act of brainstorming is calming because people are doing something natural and constructive.

later about the low grade and what I can do to improve it."

After everyone has thought of ways to manage stress, talk about how to remember to do these things in the stress of the moment. It's easy to remember them when your child doesn't need them, but when she's actually *in* that classroom, with everyone looking at her, can she remember to take a deep breath or think of a happy place (or whatever she decided will help calm her down)? One thing you can do is have your child pick out or find a little reminder object and keep it with her: a shell, a stone, a bright yellow eraser, a charm, a locket—a special little object to keep on a desk or in a pocket. That will help her remember to do what you've talked about and practiced.

Bad things happen in life that are out of our control, but we can control how we think, feel, and behave in those situations, and that's empowering. We've made this point several times throughout the book, because we believe one of the most important lessons in life is that we can choose to have negative feelings or to make the most of bad situations—to manage feelings and act like winners … or not.

Sometimes it takes some effort to manage stress—to say mantras, visualize a happy place, or go someplace private to take a calming moment. It may take some time and some energy; however, it takes a whole lot more energy to experience the stress in its raw form and not do anything about it. That's why it's important to teach children to recognize the signs and symptoms—to know when they're feeling too much stress—so they can handle it appropriately.

> It's important to teach children to recognize the signs and symptoms—to know when they're feeling too much stress—so they can handle it appropriately.

With repeated practice applying the SMART Decision Pad, your children will figure out how to not only deal with, but also anticipate and prevent harmfully stressful situations.

Notes

1. William Shakespeare, *Hamlet*. New York: Penguin Books, 1981.

2. Lori A. Leyden-Rubenstein, *Stress Management Handbook: Strategies for Health and Inner Peace*. New Canaan, CT: Keats Publishing Inc., 1998.

3. See Appendix A.

4. This technique is shown, comically but relatively accurately, in the movie *Something's Gotta Give*, when Dr. Martinez (Rachel Ticotin) helps Harry (Jack Nicholson) to "decompress": "Close your eyes. Now give yourself a visual image of something that gives you a feeling of peace and serenity."

CHAPTER 24

BE SAFE

One thing I [Jim Hawkins, a boy trapped on the deck of a ship by a wounded pirate] saw plainly: I must not simply retreat before him, or he would speedily hold me boxed into the bow, as a moment since he had so nearly boxed me in the stern. Once so caught, and nine or ten inches of the bloodstained dirk would be my last experience on this side of eternity. I placed my palms against the main-mast, which was of a goodish bigness, and waited, every nerve upon the stretch.

Seeing that I meant to dodge, he also paused; and a moment or two passed in feints upon his part, and corresponding movements upon mine. It was such a game as I had often played at home about the rocks of Black Hill Cove; but never before, you may be sure, with such a wildly beating heart as now. Still, as I say, it was a boy's game, and I thought I could hold my own at it, against an elderly seaman with a wounded thigh. Indeed, my courage had begun to rise so high that I allowed myself a few darting thoughts on what would be the end of the affair.

—*Robert Louis Stevenson*, Treasure Island[1]

NO MATTER HOW CAREFULLY PARENTS plan and how well children think, any child will occasionally encounter unsafe situations, and this worry creates a dilemma for parents: how can I protect my children without overprotecting them? The answer is that you can teach your children to protect themselves.

This chapter gives you ways to coach your children to practice anticipating, preventing, and responding to dangerous situations. As they do these activites, they will use many of the skills they've been developing in all of the other activities. When they respond to real emergencies, they will need to think fast and act effectively. Two activities will strengthen their resourcefulness and their ability to stay calm under pressure and make good decisions:

- Talk to your children about appropriate actions to take in everyday emergencies, and then practice, as a family.
- Role-play an emergency situation: hold a surprise drill and then discuss it.

Be Safe

Time: An hour initially, repeated in shorter intervals as needed.

Venue: At home.

Equipment: Depends.

Learn How to Handle Emergencies

Begin by talking about safety in general and then ask your kids how they would handle the kinds of emergencies that can come up in the best-planned lives:

- What would you do if you were home alone and heard an intruder?
- What if you were at the pool and someone was drowning? If a lifeguard was on duty? If there was no lifeguard?
- What would you do if you woke up and smelled smoke?
- What would you do if you were babysitting and heard a tornado siren?

- What would be the safest thing to do if someone tried to touch you inappropriately?
- What would you do if you got lost?
- Are there any situations like this you worry about? How would you handle them?

It's OK to have some fun. If your children have read *Treasure Island,* ask, "What would you do if you were Jim Hawkins and a one-legged pirate tried to attack you?"

Encourage your children to use the SMART Decision Pad to brainstorm and decide on solutions. *Then* offer your thoughts. After you've discussed several hypothetical situations, get specific. Teach your kids what you know about handling crises—intruders, crimes, crashes (bikes, cars), poisons, danger of drowning, or any other emergency. One client remembers how her father walked the family through putting out a fire:

We were sitting around the breakfast table one Sunday morning when my Dad walked in and out of the blue said, "OK, let's say there's a fire on the stove right now. What would you do? Where is the fire extinguisher?"

My mother knew where it was. My brother and I looked at each other, shrugged, then looked around the kitchen. We couldn't see it, so my Dad showed us where it was, "It's right here, it's in this cabinet—do you guys know how to use it?"

"Well, I can read the instructions," I said.

"Jill, you're not going to have time in an emergency to do that! So let's all gather round here and figure out how to use this thing."

So we read the instructions, saw where you flipped the little knob, flipped the trigger, and saw where to aim. It only took five minutes, but we were all glad we had done it, and even a little impressed. I remember saying at the end, "Gosh, I'm surprised we didn't know that!"

They also talked about how to call 911, get out of any of the rooms if there was a fire, and what they would take with them (if anything). Jill remembers telling her parents that she would take all her stuffed animals. Her father asked, "Is it worth getting permanent burns on your

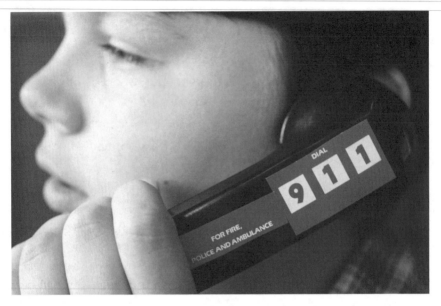

face, being scarred, or even dying, for a few stuffed animals that are made out of cotton or fake fur and plastic?" She said, "No!" and he told her, "That's right! You and your life are much more important and valuable than these objects."

These discussions help your child anticipate and avoid unsafe situations. You can go through similar drills with all the safety equipment you have in your house or car. Some families, for example, don't use their fancy alarm systems or teach their children how to use them either because they are so complicated. If you have an alarm system, teach your children how to use it; try it out, see if they can set the alarm, and then practice, saying, "If you want to set the alarm for the outside but be able to move around on the inside, what do you do? Let's see you do it."

Hold periodic updates. These are not meant as disciplinary measures or tests—you just want to make sure your children remember how to use the equipment. If your kids don't know how to do it and this is the 30th time you've practiced, do it a 31st time. Do not get upset with your children if they don't remember; it might be complicated and hard, but take the time to teach them properly.

Also take the time to let your children *earn freedom*—the freedom to enter potentially dangerous situations gradually and safely. Suppose your ten-year-old daughter wants to ride her bike to school. First, teach her about safe biking, bike with her a couple of times, and ask her questions: "What would you do if it started raining hard and a stranger with a truck offered to give you and your bike a ride home?" When the responses are sound and your daughter has demonstrated that she has enough sense to ride the bike to school safely, let her do it. Or do that gradually too. One parent told us about secretly following his daughter to school, three times, driving several hundred yards behind her, until he was sure she was safe!

Have a Surprise Drill

A surprise drill allows your children to put their knowledge into practice, just as fire drills do in school, though you won't be limiting your practice emergencies to fire drills. Begin this activity by discussing hypothetical situations and how your children would handle them. Whatever the situation, the basic reaction is to stay calm and think about what to do. (Use the SMART Decision Pad. This is using it to the max.) This activity helps your children think under pressure and practice basic survival behavior that could save their lives.

Present the drill in terms of concern for their well-being. Convey that you love and trust your children, but know that a dangerous situation can arise anywhere, at any time: "Whether we're with you or not, we love you and we want you to be safe! So we're going to practice what you would do in an emergency. You're going to act out one of those situations and handle it just the way you would handle it for real." Tell them why, too. One father said to his child, "Practicing does two things: you will have more confidence in yourself that you can handle these kinds of situations and I will feel more comfortable when I'm not with you that you know how to handle these situations."

Then give them a choice. "Sometime this week we are going to practice what you would do if something bad happened. Would you like the practice to be a surprise? That is, would you like me to wake you up in the middle of the night and say, 'Pretend you woke up because you smelled smoke!' Or I could interrupt you while you were studying and say, 'You're home alone and you hear someone moving around in the kitchen!' Or would you like us all to plan it together beforehand, so it's not a shock?" It's their choice. Then you just have to start the drama, to set the crisis in motion, and see how they handle it. You might not be there when a real emergency occurs, so really let them handle it, without any help, with no coaching. Later, after they have handled it, you can all discuss how their actions might have played out in real life, what they did well, and what they could have done differently. These realistic but staged emergencies prepare your kids to cope with crises.

As anyone who has handled a life-threatening situation successfully remembers, afterwards there is a real feeling of pride and relief, a feeling of being able to handle whatever life brings, a feeling of empowerment—and often a feeling of gratitude for having prepared. The activities in this chapter are a fraction of what you can do as a parent to equip your kids to both avoid and handle emergencies. You could all take courses in first aid, CPR, or martial arts. But first things first! This chapter deals with only the fundamentals.

The activities in this chapter help kids anticipate (to prevent) and handle (to survive) some unsafe situations. They lead to the ultimate goal of all the activities—your kids "going solo" and succeeding when you're not there. They prepare your children for leaving the nest—flying off, confident, capable, and happy with this complicated business called life. Can-do kids become can-do adults.

Does anticipating that give you a twinge of sadness? You're not alone in that. But be proud that you gave your children the best gifts a parent can give: the ability to survive and *thrive* on their own resourcefulness.

Note

1. Robert Louis Stevenson, *Treasure Island*, chapter 26. Emma Letley, editor. New York: Oxford University Press, 1988.

SMART PARENTING CASE STUDIES

P LEASE MEET TWO SMART PARENTING "poster children." Their parents never heard of "smart parenting," but instinctively raised their kids to be resourceful in all parts of their life with the hope and expectation that they would be resourceful adults and therefore become very, very happy and successful. Their hopes were fulfilled.

One "poster child" is Jack Welch, who as CEO of General Electric became the world's most respected CEO. He admits he wasn't resourceful in all aspects of his life, but he eventually fixed the missing parts. (That shows resourcefulness.) Mia Peterson has Down syndrome, but because her parents coached her to make smart decisions, she now lives independently. See if you don't find their stories inspiring!

Jack Welch: The Most Respected CEO

After 20 years as chairman and CEO of General Electric, the most respected company in the world, Jack Welch retired. In poll after poll conducted by leading business magazines, Jack for years was ranked #1, the most respected CEO, not just in the United States, but world-

wide, and he is a legendary leader. As a consultant to GE, contributing to talent assessment and development programs, I (Brad) witnessed firsthand Jack's unparalleled resourcefulness in transforming GE from bureaucratic to agile, from "OK with talent" to "loaded with A players." How did he become so resourceful?

Jack was reared in a working-class neighborhood of Salem, Massachusetts. His father, a railroad conductor, was an excellent role model, showing Jack responsibility, honesty, hard work, and the importance of trying to do one's best. If there was bad weather, he would ask Jack's mother to drive him to the station the night before, so he could sleep in one of the cars and be ready for work the next morning. He collected newspapers from the cars at the end of the day and took them home, encouraging young Jack to read. At six years of age, Jack was a voracious reader, and his thirst for knowledge has never abated. His father was not formally educated but knew Jack would progress faster if he learned everything he could.

Jack's mother Grace, however, was the most influential person in building his can-do attitude. He was an only child, born when his mother was 36 years of age and, as he put it, "My mother poured her love into me as if I were a found treasure." Instead of a silver spoon placed in his mouth, he had two loving parents and Irish immigrant grandparents to rear him; from this extended family Jack says he received "tons of love." In his autobiography, *Jack: Straight from the Gut*, Jack says of his mother, "If I have any leadership style, a way of getting the best out of people, I owe it to her. Tough and aggressive, warm and generous, she was a great judge of character. ... And many of my basic management beliefs—things like competing hard to win, facing reality, motivating people by alternately hugging and kicking them, setting stretch goals, and relentlessly following up on people to make sure things get done—can be traced to her as well." Jack's mother had very high expectations for him. She said, "If you don't study, you'll be nothing. Absolutely nothing. There are no shortcuts. Don't kid yourself!" If Jack screwed up, there would be hell to pay, always within the context of his feeling totally loved. She was a tough, stern disciplinarian. Her style was tough love, with a lot of tough and a lot more love.

Jack's mother inspired his resourcefulness. She pushed him to take day trips on his own, so that he would learn to figure things out by himself with no one to hold his hand. She didn't overprotect him. She knew his safety and happiness required him to become streetwise and savvy. He feels that the single greatest gift she gave him was self-confidence. One of the hallmarks of his tenure as CEO was to build self-confidence in executives, not with hollow praise or false pats on the back, but with hard-headed confrontation of reality, an occasional kick in the pants, but always an inspiring pep talk or note that conveyed, "I know you can do this!" His mother built his self-confidence by turning weaker points into strengths. He has stammered all his life and only in recent years got therapy to deal with it. His mother would say that his brain was too fast for his tongue; that was a comforting explanation, protecting his ego. When he would fall down, Jack would be expected to pick himself up, but if he needed an extra boost, she was there. Her "go for it!" attitude has always been

> She didn't overprotect him. She knew his safety and happiness required him to become streetwise and savvy.

an inspiration to him. She was an energized doer, and Jack couldn't help but copy her spirit.

Though Jack's mother was the disciplinarian with very high expectations for him, they also played together. He recalls running home from grammar school at noon to have lunch and play gin rummy with her. She knew a key principle of resourcefulness parenting: build and maintain a positive relationship, so that your child will want to spend time with you, will respect discipline, and won't want to disappoint you.

The portrait Jack Welch paints of his mother is one of a parent who wanted the very best for her child and was willing to invest hours and hours every day in him. However, she instinctively knew not to smother or overprotect him, and that he must learn to figure things out on his own. She did not overcontrol or promote dependency in Jack, but was truly delighted when he would grow, achieve, and make smart decisions. In her own unique way, this scrappy and generous woman had mastered resourcefulness parenting!

Mia Peterson, Independent Businesswoman with Down Syndrome

If you had a child with Down syndrome, would you load her up with do's and don'ts and make important decisions for her, or would you help her develop as a can-do kid? Mia Peterson's parents, Mike and Carol, did both, with the major emphasis on helping Mia become resourceful and capable of making good decisions on her own. They succeeded as parents and Mia has succeeded in life. Instead of being institutionalized or under constant watch, Mia became a can-do adult and now lives independently. Book-smart kids may be quicker to use the SMART Decision Pad, but the results aren't necessarily better. Her story can inspire every parent and child.

In 1997, Mia left her parents in Iowa and moved to Cincinnati to live by herself, physically far from her parents in Iowa but emotionally close. She worked at Capabilities Unlimited Inc. as Self-Advocacy Coordinator and President and then as Advocacy Support Specialist for a county board of mental retardation and developmental disabilities.

Mia is a delightful, articulate, engaging person, which makes her very effective as a professional. And she is an entrepreneur. Her terrific reputation as a speaker led to more and more requests, so she created Aiming High, Inc., a budding public relations and training firm. Mia is a co-facilitator, working with a certified trainer with a version of Stephen Covey's book, *The 7 Habits of Highly Successful People,* designed for people with disabilities. These various sources of income make her almost financially independent.

Mia is the first person with Down syndrome to be named to the Board of Directors of the National Down Syndrome Society and has been President of People First of Ohio, a self-advocacy organization. She testified before the U.S. Senate on the 10th anniversary of the Americans with Disabilities Act. Her accomplishments continue to accumulate, for her contributions connecting those with disabilities to the rest of the world are so real. In 2005 Mia moved to Des Moines, Iowa, to work as the Assistant to Support Staff at Iowa Protection and Advocacy Services, Inc., where she is also editor of an internal staff newsletter. She currently serves on the board for the National Down Syndrome Society, for which she is chair and editor for the Advocacy Advisory Board.

How did Mia become so savvy, street smart, and resourceful? The short answer is that her parents instinctively knew that resourcefulness would be key to her success and happiness in life, as a kid and later as an adult. So they coached her to become a can-do kid. Very humble people, the Petersons explain that Mia was lucky enough to possess God-given talents in energy, verbal skills, judgment, insight into people, and irrepressible perseverance. They feel Mia was lucky to grow up in a wonderful small town where people accepted her. Though Mike and Carol were encouraged by professionals to protect or even overprotect Mia, instead they lovingly coached her to take risks, to grow and stretch, and to make decisions on her own. They recall that since her early childhood, Mia not only wanted to do things on her own, but insisted on it, so their influence was to guide her without diminishing her zest for life.

Mia has always been fond of her two sisters, an older one who has been a role model she could never keep up with, and a younger sister she loves but always tried to stay ahead of. The result of this rivalry was a lot of "Mommy, I want to do it myself." If her younger sister would tie her own shoes, Mia was determined to tie hers and sat on the front steps for a day attempting, failing, attempting, failing, and finally succeeding. Her parents encouraged her without offering a lot of advice, because Mia wanted to figure it out herself.

> "Mommy, I want to do it myself."

Later, Mia wanted to sing in choir, but failed the audition. Her parents' gentle message was "Try hard to pursue your goals, figure out how to overcome obstacles, but move on if you don't succeed." Mia moved on, sort of. Her next singing goal was to perform "The Star Spangled Banner" before basketball games. Her parents coached her through an informal decision-making model, identifying some major obstacles like a "so-so" voice and lack of voice training. Mia figured out a way to train herself—karaoke. Devoting a full month to practicing, she then got several opportunities to sing the National Anthem at Special Olympics Opening Ceremonies. Finding a solution herself was far more satisfying than if her parents had hired a voice coach or simply discouraged her from trying. And it helped her become independent.

Mia has always wanted to be a writer. Today, writing is an important part of her job and she is writing a book. She also has recorded a song, "I Am Here," a poem that she wrote that was put to music. As a teenager she applied for a position as sports writer of the local newspaper, but was turned down. Mia would write something, hoping to get an article, a letter, or anything published in the community press, and she would ask her parents, "Is it good enough?" Their typical response was "It's not bad for a draft, but probably needs some work for publication." They might say, "By the end of the article I've forgotten your main points," and Mia might say, "I need a summary at the end." She worked hard to develop writing skills and later public speaking skills, finally distinguishing herself as a national spokeswoman.

Along this developmental journey, Mia's parents and other caring adults (like Essie Pederson of Capabilities Unlimited Inc., her mentor) participated in developing Mia's can-do spirit, long before this book was conceived. Informally, those adults did the equivalent of many of the activities in this book. They would sometimes make some suggestions, but typically leave room for Mia to clarify her own goal and evaluate options on her own. Because they did not overprotect and stifle Mia, her motivation remained high and so she constantly readjusted goals and tried to figure out options that would lead to success. Small successes reinforced Mia's irrepressible drive, and with bigger successes, her resourcefulness expanded. With each decision Mia made, her resourcefulness grew and she became a little better equipped to truly run her own life.

Mia has applied her version of the SMART Decision Pad in all aspects of her life. She has had help, with adults reinforcing that model again and again. She has participated in numerous youth leadership conferences, typically devoting most of a week to helping peers to set goals, weigh various options, and implement plans. So, professionally she is training others with disabilities to develop their decision-making "smarts."

The transition from living at home in Iowa to living independently in Cincinnati involved plenty of decision making for Mia, and she was coached by many adults. Mia's several caring mentors and many loving family members have helped her solve problems in career, personal finances, relationships, wellness, and spiritual realms. Their combined genius has been not in making many decisions for Mia, but in coaching her to make good choices herself—and "so far so good." She has never been seriously injured or hurt although she's been physically active, working out at the local YMCA and running, swimming, biking, and taking classes in Powerstrike (an exercise technique similar to kickboxing). She continues to add achievements to her long list of impressive accomplishments.

Mia's optimistic, "go for it!" attitude is conveyed in her recently using a decision-making model to create a career plan. Her goal is to expand her public relations firm that serves the disadvantaged. She has a written plan she is implementing. In talking with Mia, we somehow cannot help but feel that she will be successful, that if the plan doesn't go perfectly she'll be flexible and persistent—creating her own successes. Mia Peterson is a winner in the game of life and happy that her parents gave her the skills to become a can-do adult.

RESOURCE GUIDE
AND REFERENCES

F YOU WONDER IF YOUR CHILD NEEDS professional help, we suggest discussing the situation with your child's health care provider. He or she may refer your child to a counselor, psychologist, psychiatrist, or some other mental health professional who can do a thorough evaluation and offer appropriate treatment. It can also be beneficial to educate yourself on various mental issues and/or disorders as they relate to your child. We recommend getting professional help when any of the following is true of your child:

■ Symptoms cause significant distress or impairment in academic, social, family, or other important situations, and efforts to remedy the symptom have failed.

■ Symptoms or disturbances cause significant change in your child's eating, sleeping, or daily behavior.

■ You suspect your child has suicidal or violent thoughts or your child has voiced these thoughts.

Following are four general resources offering hard copy and online articles, books, brochures, and sources of professional help.

National Mental Health Association (NMHA)

The National Mental Health Association is the country's oldest and largest nonprofit organization addressing all aspects of mental health and mental illness. With more than 340 affiliates nationwide, NMHA works to improve the mental health of all Americans, especially the 54 million people with mental disorders, through advocacy, education, research and service.

NMHA offers:

- Suicide hot line (1-800-SUICIDE)
- Brochures, free, on more than 60 mental health topics
- Answers to questions such as how to find mental health therapy services

Contact Information

National Mental Health Association
2001 N. Beauregard Street, 12th Floor
Alexandria, VA 22311
Phone: 703-684-7722
Fax: 703-684-5968
Mental Health Resource Center: 800-969-NMHA
TTY Line: 800-433-5959
Web site: www.NMHA.org

National Institute of Mental Health (NIMH)

NIMH is the lead Federal agency for research on mental and behavioral disorders. The organization has a strong commitment to educating the public, providing the latest research-based information. NIMH offers health information on:

- Anxiety Disorders
- Attention Deficit Hyperactivity Disorder (ADHD, ADD)
- Autism Spectrum Disorders (Pervasive Developmental Disorders)
- Bipolar Disorder (Manic-Depressive Illness)
- Borderline Personality Disorder
- Depression
- Eating Disorders

- Generalized Anxiety Disorder
- Obsessive-Compulsive Disorder (OCD)
- Panic Disorder
- Post-Traumatic Stress Disorder (PTSD)
- Schizophrenia
- Social Phobia (Social Anxiety Disorder)

Contact Information
> National Institute of Mental Health (NIMH)
> Public Information and Communications Branch
> 6001 Executive Boulevard, Room 8184, MSC 9663
> Bethesda, MD 20892-9663
> Phone (local): 301-443-4513
> Phone (toll-free): 866-615-6464
> TTY (local): 301-443-8431
> TTY (toll-free): 866-415-8051
> Fax: 301-443-4279
> E-mail: NIMHinfo@nih.gov

American Psychological Association (APA)

The American Psychological Association is a scientific and professional association representing 150,000 psychologists. It is the largest association of psychologists worldwide. APA's Help Center is an online resource for brochures, tips, and articles on the psychological issues that affect people's physical and emotional well-being, as well as information about referrals.

Contact Information
> American Psychological Association
> 750 First Street, NE
> Washington, DC 20002-4242
> Phone: 800-374-5600
> TDD/TTY: 202-336-6123
> Web site: http://www.apa.org
> APA Help Center Web site: www.apahelpcenter.org

Psych Central

Dr. John Grohol's Psych Central advertises that it is the "oldest anno-tated directory of online psychology and mental health resources," dating back to 1992. The Web site offers almost 4,000 resources in the following categories:

- Abuse
- Alcoholism and Substance Abuse
- Alzheimer Disease and Dementia
- Anxiety and Panic
- Articles and Essays
- Attention Deficit Disorder
- Bipolar Disorder
- Books (reviews of dozens of books)
- Depression
- Disability
- Dissociation
- Eating Disorders
- Grief and Loss
- Health and Wellness
- Licensing Information
- Medical Disease Support
- Medications
- Mental Health
- Obsessive-Compulsive Disorder
- Parents and Children Issues
- Personality Disorders
- Post-Traumatic Stress
- Psychotherapy
- Relationship Issues
- Schizophrenia and Psychosis

- Sexual and Gender Issues
- Suicide and Crisis

Contact Information

Web site: www.psychcentral.com

INDEX

A

Achievement, 9–10, 37. *See also* High achievers
Active listening
  activities for, 130–135
  elements of, 128–129
  tips for parents, 14, 35–36
Acts of kindness, 174–178
Adult club leaders, 159
Advance notice, 59
Advice, excessive, 5, 7
Age, moral development and, 86–87
Aiming High, Inc., 211
Alarm systems, 204
Allowances, 181–182
Altruism, 174–178
American Psychological Association, 217
Anger control, 196
Anticipation, 168–172
APA Help Center, 217
Arguments, 45–46
Articles, discussing at meals, 46

B

Behavior, as emphasis in discipline, 83
Body language
  children's cues from, 44–45
  to demonstrate listening, 133–135
  facial expressions, 131
Books, 79
Bossidy, Larry, 158

Brainstorming
  to achieve goals, 21–23
  building activities, 69–70
  family volunteer projects, 175
  problem prevention, 170
  stress management, 197–199
  tips for parents, 13, 24
Branson, Richard, 106
Breaks, while learning together, 62
Brobst, Stephen, 58
Broken windows, 77–78, 79–80
Bubblegum in hair, 78–79
Budgeting, 179–182
Building activities
  brainstorming, 69–70
  completing, 72–74
  overview, 67–69
  planning, 70–72
Bullying, 22–23, 24
Bus bullies, 22–23, 24
Businesses, starting, 155–157

C

Cabin visits
  major benefits, 96–100
  preparing for, 100–101
  rules for, 101–104
Capabilities Unlimited Inc., 210
Car contracts, 93, 94
Case studies
  Jack Welch, 207–210
  Mia Peterson, 210–214

Charitable donations, 182
Cheating story, 84–85
Cheerleading, 14
Chess playing, 57–58
Chores during getaways, 100
Clubs, leading, 157–160
Coaching, 158
Comfort zones, stretching, 151–152
Comparisons, avoiding, 63
Compound interest, 184–186
Conflict resolution, 149
Consequences
    following through with, 92–95
    having child suggest, 87, 89–90
    importance of, 85
Consultative selling, 130
Conversation
    about investing, 188
    after team activities, 152–153
    encouraging during meals, 42–48
    teaching children to initiate,
        122–127
Corcoran, Meg, 71–72, 73, 74
Creativity, 7
Crises, 119–120, 202–205
Crockett, Davy, 82
Cultural differences, 124

D

Dangerous situations, 202–206
Decision making, 14, 19. *See also*
    SMART Decision Pad
Dependence, 6
Dinners. *See* Meals together
Discipline
    discussions with child, 86–92
    fact finding, 83–86
    following through, 92–95
    overview, 82–83
Discoveries during getaways,
    102–103
Disorders, mental, 215
Dog walking, 176

Drake, Ann, 19
Drills, 205–206
Driving contracts, 93, 94

E

Earhart, Amelia, 67–68, 69
Earning freedom, 205
Earning money, 182
Electronic games, 101
Emergencies, 202–205
Empathy, 119–120, 131
Encouragement, 62–64, 73. *See also*
    Praise
Ethics, discussing, 47–48. *See also*
    Moral values
Evaluation, in decision-making
    model, 23–24
Expenses, budgeting, 179–182

F

Facial expressions, 131
Fact finding, for discipline, 83–86
Failure, accepting, 15
Faith in children, displaying, 15
Fifteen-minute reminders, 59
Fires, 203–204
First impressions, 123
Fisher, Bobby, 57
Fish feeder, 69–70
Fixing things
    letting child decide, 76–78
    overview, 75–76
    research, 78–81
Flight cancellations, 191
Following through on discipline,
    92–95
Food, shopping for, 180–181. *See also*
    Meals together
Forcing decisions on children, 28–29
Foresight, 168–172
Freedom, earning, 205
Friends, identifying with, 116–117
Friendships, 99–100, 136–141
Frontier House, 102
Fun, importance of, 15

G

Generosity, 174–178
Getaways. *See* Vacations
Gliders, 55–57
Goals
    ethical, 47
    helping children to form, 21
    leaders' focus on, 158
    for teams, 149
Grocery shopping, 180–181
Grohol, John, 218

H

Habitat for Humanity, 176
Handshakes, 123, 125
Healthy responses to stress, 197–198
Helplessness, encouraging, 5–6
High achievers
    active listening by, 129
    attributes of, 9–10
    family mealtime experience, 37
    vacation experiences, 97
Horses, 55
How Kids Make Friends, 138
Humor, 44, 196
Hypothetical investments, 186–187

I

Ideas for building activities, 69–70
Imaginary illness, 193–194
Incentives for self-discipline, 93
Initiative, suppressing, 6–7
Interest, compound, 184–186
Interest levels, checking, 60–61
Interjections, 132–133
Internet
    investment tools, 185, 186–187
    research on, 78–79
Interruptions, avoiding during meal-
    times, 41–42
Introducing oneself, 122–127
Investing, 183–188

K

Kindness, demonstrating, 174–178

L

Laughter at mealtimes, 44
Leadership
    active listening in, 129
    activities to develop, 154–160
    learning, 104
Learning styles, 60
Learning together
    allowing time, 59
    checking interest level, 60–61
    choosing activities, 54–58
    general tips, 53–54
    modeling, 61–62
    perseverance, 64–66
    praise and encouragement, 62–64
Lemonade stands, 17, 156
Listening
    active listening activities, 128–135
    good and bad examples, 33–34
    importance of, 14
    modeling good behavior, 61
Lochner, Jim, 53
Looking ahead, 168–172
Losers and winners, 161–166

M

Making light of problems, 196
Manners, 48, 122–127
Maps, 111
MarineMax, 19
Marital counseling, listening in, 129
Marvel Entertainment, 187
McGill, Bill, 12, 18–19
Meals, budgeting for, 180–181
Meals together
    encouraging conversation, 42–48
    main purpose, 38–39
    manners during, 48
    relation to achievement, 37
    scheduling and planning, 39–42
Meeting and greeting people,
    122–127
Mental health organizations,
    215–217

Menus, 41
Metropolitan Boating Club, 54
Michelle, Lonnie, 138
Modeling behavior
    parental arguments, 45–46
    table manners, 48
    while learning together, 61–62
Money management
    budgeting, 179–182
    investing, 183–188
Moral values
    age-appropriate approaches,
        86–87
    discipline and, 85
    discussing at mealtimes, 47–48
    importance of consequences,
        94–95
Movies, 4

N

National Down Syndrome Society,
    211, 212
National Institute of Mental Health,
    216–217
National Mental Health
    Association, 216
Navigation activities
    finding routes, 107–111
    planning trips, 111–114
Negative parenting, 8
Nonverbal communication. *See*
    Body language

O

Observing winners and whiners,
    163–166
Officers, leaders versus, 157
Olsen, Tim, 186
On-the-fly speeches, 145–146
Open-ended questions, 43
Opinions, encouraging, 35, 43
Options, assessing, 21–23
Overprotection
    impact on self-reliance, 5, 7–8
    importance of avoiding, 14, 202

Oxfam, 174

P

Parental arguments, 45–46
Passivity, 5
Patience with child's decision mak-
    ing, 14
Pederson, Essie, 213
People First of Ohio, 211
Perseverance, 64–66
Peterson, Mia, 207, 210–214
Physical signs of stress, 193
Planning
    building activities, 70–72
    meals, 40–42
    trips, 111–114
Positive parenting, 8–9
Positive self-talk, 195–196
Positive stress, 190
Practice
    with emergency systems,
        203–206
    meeting and greeting people,
        124–126
    for public speaking, 143
Praise
    during building activities, 73
    for having commendable quali-
        ties, 137
    for public speaking, 143–144
    sincere, 24
    while learning together, 62–63, 64
Problem prevention, 168–172
Professional resources, 215–219
Protection from harm, 202–206
Psych Central, 218–219
Public speaking, 142–146
Punishments
    following through with, 92–95
    having child suggest, 87, 89–90

Q

Questioning
    in decision-making model, 21
    to encourage conversation, 42–43

tips for parents, 14
in visualization, 194–195

R

Rational approach to discipline, 91
Relaxation techniques, 194–196
Reminder objects, 199
Repairs. *See* Fixing things
Repeating stories, 132–133
Research, 78–81
Resourcefulness, 4–5, 9–10
Rest breaks, 62
Rock-throwing incident, 88–91
Role models. *See* Modeling behavior
Role-playing, 124–126
Roles on teams, 149
Ropes courses, 150–152
Routes, finding, 107–111
Rules, 86, 101–104

S

Safety, 202–206
Saving, 182, 183–188
Scarlet fever, 193–194
Seating at meals, 40
Seeing yourself on video, 117–118
Self-confidence, 209
Self-discovery, 102–103
Selfishness, avoiding, 174–178
Self-perceptions, 115–120
Self-protection, 202–206
Self-talk, positive, 195–196
Selling, consultative, 130
Sentence completion, 197
Sharing food, 174
Sharing the floor, 44–45
SMART Decision Pad
    basic implementation, 24–31
    in emergencies, 205
    glider example, 56
    for making friends, 138
    problem prevention with, 171–172
    for social crises, 119
    steps in, 20–24
    use in stress management, 198

Smart Parenting equation, 10
Smart Parenting model, 11
Smart Parenting tips, 13–15
Softball, 25–27
Spassky, Boris, 57
Speaking in public, 142–146
Special touches at family meals, 41
Speculating, investing versus, 186
Spending money, 179–182
Stain removal, 77
Steak sauce, 44
Stealing, 91–92
Sticking with learning, 64–66
Storytelling, 132–133
Stress
    children's sensitivity to, 34
    common sources, 190–191
    healthy responses to, 194–199
    recognizing, 192–194
Study, in decision-making model, 21
Suicide hot line, 216
Sunday dinner, 39
Surprise drills, 205–206
Swallows and Amazons, 96, 104–105
Symptoms of mental disorders, 215

T

Table decorations, 41
Table manners, 48
Take 10 exercise, 196
Taking breaks, 62
Taking stock, 23–24
Teamwork, 147–153
The Teenage Investor, 184, 186
Telephones, avoiding during meal-
    times, 42
Television, 4, 41
Thinking ahead, 168–172
Thinking skills, 46
Threats, avoiding, 63
Time, investing, 10–13, 59
Toys, creative, 7
Trip planning, 111–114
Trust, demonstrating, 113–114

U

Unconditional love, 15
Unhealthy responses to stress,
   197–198
Unsafe situations, 202–206
Unstructured time, 4, 103–104

V

Vacations
   major benefits, 96–100
   preparing for, 100–101
   rules for, 101–104
Values
   age-appropriate approaches,
      86–87
   discipline and, 85
   discussing at mealtimes, 47–48
   importance of consequences,
      94–95

Video, imagining oneself on,
   117–118
Videotaping a speech, 143–144
Visualization, 194–195
Volunteering, 174–178

W

Web sites
   investment tools, 185, 186–187
   psychological issues, 217,
      218–219
   using for research, 78–79
Welch, Jack, 15, 207–210
Window repairs, 77–78, 79–80
Winners and whiners, 161–166
Writing skills, 213

Z

Zambian Exchange Club, 159–160

About the Authors

Dr. Brad Smart is a world-renowned psychologist specializing in developing the talents of people in organizations. He is author of four books, including the bestselling *Topgrading: How Leading Companies Win By Hiring, Coaching, and Keeping The Best People* (Portfolio, 2005).

Dr. Kate Smart Mursau is a family therapist. Her doctoral dissertation showed resourcefulness to be a highly valuable life skill, and that few parents develop resourcefulness in their children.

Visit their Web site at **www.AskSmartParenting.com**.